A GREAT FIGHT
IS A PRODUCT OF
GREAT FAITH

WILFRED A. BROWN

© 2021 Divine Works Publishing

GREAT FIGHT IS A PRODUCT OF GREAT FAITH

All rights reserved. No part of this publication may be reproduced, stored in a retrieval system, or transmitted in any form or by any means, electronic, mechanical, photocopying, recording or otherwise without the prior permission of the publisher or in accordance with the provisions of the Copyright, Designs, and Patents Act 1988 or under the terms of any license permitting limited copying issued by the Copyright Licensing Agency.

The views expressed in this work are solely those of the author and do not necessarily reflect the views of the publisher, the publisher hereby disclaims any responsibility for them.

Art Work Special Credits to Raoel Tjaaroeme and Womack.

ISBN-13: 978-1-949105-41-4 (paperback)
ISBN-13: 978-1-949105-43-8 (hardback)
ISBN-13: 978-1-949105-42-1 (eBook)

Published by:
Divine Works Publishing
Royal Palm Beach, Florida USA
561-990-BOOK (2665)
www.DivineWorksPublishing,com

DEDICATION

I thank God for my wife,
Inga Hendrickson-Brown

*I don't know what I did to deserve you.
God has blessed me with the ninth wonder of the world;
you are a beautiful treasure. You are the most humble,
god-fearing, loving, kind, caring, beautiful woman I ever
met. You are my heartbeat, my biggest cheerleader, my
biggest fan, my soul-mate, my wife, the one I would die for.
Thank you for all your love and support;
I couldn't do this without you.
I LOVE YOU FOR LIFE!*

POEM: WE WIN

Through the pages of time from that great book foretold
A battle will take place between the righteous
and the forces of darkness
A spiritual battle where the true warriors will stand strong,
fully armed to fight

We all knew this day would come
It was foreseen
It was foretold and now is
Wait... and now is?

With the realization of a monstrosity of a collision
about to take place
Only then does it sink in that practice has here and now come
to a screeching halt.

As time seems to hold the hour, minute, second hands
all together in the tightest of grip.
Releasing just enough for us to dress up, show out show
what we are made up of

Show what we've been training for yearly, monthly, daily,
even down to this very second
We were taught by some of the best scholars,
To know every battle move had to be met with swift
and precise accuracy

Every swing of the sword had to release a surge of energy
Proclaiming victory and never ever defeat
No second-guessing
This armor, has been prayed into its spiritual place
Yes, in practice on our knees is where we now salute proudly
Our battle cry to stand for Christ and his heavenly army

As the storm grows in the East and powers in the darkest
seem to gain ground in the West
God's army sharpens, deepens its spiritual growth
by reinforcing the breastplate of righteousness
through that Holy of Holies Book
Yeah, you know the one
Where the words engrained say we're not to do battle
Against our brother, sister or even our neighbor

Why, you may ask?
Because this battle is not a physical boxing match
No, this battle surges into the depth of a demonic
underground world which is why
We haven't the time for wishy washy preachers
who tend to shy away from the full gospel
of Jesus Christ

You know, the ones who skip over it like sheep jumping a fence

Why?
Because there's plenty of time to come back and train
Sidelining the reality that heaven and hell
are just as real as you and I
Preaching around the fact that there are real forces
after our souls
Evil sources that want us dead
Yes, dead, not to mention caught in sin
in order to join a never ending fiery pit

So, in this battle as we collide our Lord goes before us
and will fight for us
But it's our spiritual right to know our enemy's weakness
And yes do kick him while he's down
Remind the enemy that his position still lies under our feet
Remember, this is a fixed fight where God and His hosts
are the ultimate winners

Why?
Because we never lose
We always triumph over principalities, against powers,
against the rulers of the darkness of this world,

against spiritual wickedness in high places.
Our God always leads his chosen people into victory

Never defeat!
And God also promises that to His Kingdom
there will be no end
As we grow in numbers and in strength
We refuse to back down
We choose to advance and gain ground
On our enemy's fleeting army
Who knows his time is quickly coming to an inevitable end

Why?
Because we are fortified and covered
By the blood of Jesus Christ
We march into battle renewed in our minds
With our feet prepared with the gospel of peace
Holding high the blood stained banner of righteousness
We earnestly pray for lost souls to make the right choice
And enlarge our father's territory
We choose as Christian soldiers to fight side by side
To send a strong message to this world
That Jesus Christ is the true and living King

What a shout!
A great shout of victory in Heaven and on earth
A jubilant shout knowing that our God has heard our plea,
Our prayer in sincerity
And one more soul was snatched from death into a life of victory
Yes! Jesus Christ has won!

Based on Ephesians 6:10-20
Written by: Inga Hendrickson-Brown

COVENANT

My life is a creation of God's Promises. On my journey, I have had to learn to count on His promises. As I write this book, I am discovering how God's promises are much like a binding oath. God knows all of my struggles, weaknesses, and fears, which is why I believe He led me to the book of Hebrews.

In the book of Hebrews, you see God's word as more than a mere promise and instead as a binding oath wherein when people commit, they call on someone greater than themselves to hold them to it. So Hebrews 6 tells us that God also bound Himself with an oath so that we could be confident that He would never change His mind.

My covenant with God is a two-way promise that began at the age of fourteen, when I got baptized. As an adult, I learned that His blessings are not dependent on my worthiness, but on His grace and the forgiving love of Jesus Christ. I received blessings even when I thought I didn't deserve them. His covenant is the reason why, and understanding covenants is a lifelong process. The covenant of God I genuinely love is found in Isaiah 41:10 *"Fear not, for I am with you; be not dismayed, for I am your God; I will strengthen you, I will help you, I will uphold you with my righteous right hand."*

CONTENTS

Chapter 1 Reviewing the Journey, See the Vision | 1

Chapter 2 Designing Your Destiny | 13

Chapter 3 The Danger of Knowledge | 21

Chapter 4 Mastering the Art of Manifestation | 33

Chapter 5 Heroes are Made from Fiery Battles | 41

Chapter 6 Proven Strategies for Success | 51

Chapter 7 Build Your Dream Board | 59

Chapter 8 Cultivate Purposeful Living | 67

Chapter 9 Create Change by Raising Your Standards | 73

Chapter 10 Fighting the Good Fight of Faith | 81

Chapter 11 Pay Attention! | 91

Chapter 12 Choosing the Truth| 97

Chapter 13 Marriage: Living Happily Ever After | 103

Chapter 14 Ministry: The Great Commission | 111

Chapter 15 The Seasons of Sowing and Reaping | 117

A Prayer for Your Great Fight | 123

About the Author | 125

ACKNOWLEDGMENTS

I thank God daily for my wife and our three beautiful children Jaleena, Leanna, and Michael; they are our gems.

A heart-felt thanks goes out to all the Spiritual Leaders, whose wisdom has taught me faith and hope. You have inspired me throughout my journey. Your leadership helped me to discover my purpose and identity.

To my brothers, Adrian, Kevin, Richard, and Castle, growing up with you guys was an adventure, but we made it through! I love you guys.

To my mother, Velore Stone, your prayers have carried me through some tough times in life. I love you forever.

To my extended family Mr. Theophilius and Mrs. Jane Hendrickson, thank you for your support, assistance, and prayers. Your prayers and consistency carried me through to the completion of this book.

To my brother and sister from another mother, Mr. Raoel and Gersha Tjaaroeme. I appreciate the long hours and late nights you invested in making this book a reality. Thank you from the bottom of my heart, my success is your success. Much love always!

THANK YOU, LORD!

    I thank God for His everlasting love and His presence that has never left my side. I thank You, Lord, for everything You have taken me through, while always reminding me that You have been by my side from the day I was born. Thanks for giving me the confidence and a heart to never quit no matter what the circumstance, or despite what people may say or do. Thanks for the Holy Spirit that lives in me. Whenever I strayed, you did not leave me or forsake me. Thank You for the continuing courage to stand up every time I fall, to stand even when I don't know where I am going.

    For all the times when I wasn't sure I was going to make it, Thank you, Lord, for never giving up on me. When I felt no one loved me, thank You for showing me Your love. Your goodness and mercy have brought me through.

PERSONAL MISSION

My mission is to help people by empowering them to live their best life now. "Change your mind, change your life" is a phrase I love to use. I also find pleasure in mentoring young people and business owners.

"The change will not come if we wait for some other person or some other time. We are the ones we've been waiting for. We are the change that we seek." -Barack Obama

Our future is shaped by what we believe, the values we hold dear, the decisions we make, the values we stand for, and the character we live by.

The Bible says: *As a man/woman thinks, so is he/she. Proverbs 23:7,* where we start in life, does not determine where we will end up. I believe the difficulty of our individual struggles can inspire us to greater heights. I have been inspired by everything I've been through. By dreaming a better dream, I ended up in a place I never thought I would be.

INTRODUCTION

This book, *Great Fight is a product of Great Faith*, focuses on life's journey, the lessons taught, and the lessons learned. It is the pursuit of a seed or a word planted in our hearts that tells us that we can become whatever we dream. It's about a decision to believe in God and trust him with your life.

This book is written to inspire those of us who chose to believe they can become great or better than what the naysayers say we are.

We hope that this book will inspire you to believe that you can take a simple idea or concept and bring it forth from the supernatural into the natural. It's the pursuit to become all that God calls us to be. It's merely to fulfill a purpose. The spirit in us reminds us that we are warriors, fighters, and must never give up and never back down, because GREATER is HE that is in us than he that's against us (1 John 4:4 NIV). So let us pick up our sword—the Word of God, and our shield of Faith and fight for our dreams.

CHAPTER 1

REVIEWING THE JOURNEY, SEE THE VISION

If a prophet told you God said to put your affairs in order, that you were going to die—just like the Prophet Isaiah did, upon approaching King Hezekiah in 2 Kings 20 v1, when he announced, *"Thus says the Lord: set your house in order, for you shall die and not live."* How would you live? What would you do?

I had to face this question when I was 23 years old and attended a life changing seminar. The instructor asked us to write our obituaries as an exercise in self-discovery. The session was designed to help us become fully aware of who we were and to help us consciously decide what we wanted our lives to be like.

The inspiration behind this exercise was that Alfred Nobel, the man who founded the Nobel Prize, was reading a newspaper one day, when to his surprise, he turned the page to discover his obituary inside. It turns out that his brother had died, and the newspaper had mistakenly published it as his obituary instead. In that moment, Mr. Nobel had a moment of sheer clarity as he pondered on how the world would remember him after his death.

It is believed that due to this shock, Alfred Nobel decided to set aside the bulk of his estate to establish the *Nobel Foundation*, which annually bestows international awards in recognition of cultural and scientific advances. Alfred Nobel was a Swedish chemist who held 355 different patents—dynamite, being his most famous. Today, Alfred is not remembered as the merchant of death, but as the creator of the Nobel Prizes and consequently, as a great humanitarian. Having read his obituary while he was still alive allowed him to purposefully affect his legacy.

Although it sounds a bit morbid, writing your obituary or asking a friend or a family member to do it for you can be an excellent wake-up call to help make essential changes in your life.

ACTIVITY:

Write your obituary as an accurate account of your life to date. As an alternative, if you want to be more objective, you can ask a friend or family member who knows you well to do it for you. Whenever they are finished, find a quiet place to look over the information and ask yourself questions such as:

- *If I died today, would I die satisfied with what I have done so far with my life?*
- *Am I satisfied with the direction in which my life is headed?*
- *Am I happy with the legacy that I'm creating?*
- *What's missing from my life?*

After you finish reading, write a fantasy obituary where you write down everything you wish you had done with your life. What does this exercise tell you? You're not dead yet, so get out there and start making any changes that you need to so that you can start "living up" to your fantasy obituary. Look at yourself in the mirror, and be honest, and ask yourself whether or not you are living the life you are called to live. Are you fulfilling your purpose, are you fulfilling God's call on your life? Are you ready to fight the great fight of faith for your future?

God is a God of purpose, everything that God created, he created with a purpose. Therefore, you must never be afraid to dream big, and if you desire to do something great, nothing is impossible, and most importantly, nothing is impossible with God.

CHILDHOOD PRECURSORS

When I was growing up, I was voted by my family most likely to never succeed, to never become anyone that people would look up to. Everything they did, the words they often spoke, were degrading or discouraging. One of my family members coined a nickname that was placed upon me, "*big worthless.*" It stuck for a while, because they did not see any potential in me, they never encouraged me to excel, and they pushed me toward school courses which required more physical ability, or should I say, more technical than academic aptitude.

As a child, I battled with what is termed today as *Attention Deficit Hyperactivity Disorder* or *ADHD*. Because of this, they referred to me as a troublesome child. Needless to say, I became the recipient of lots of punishment (*the saying to justify this all was "spare the rod and spoil the child"*).

I was dragged to the doctor's office by my great-grandmother who inquired if there was an injection or a cure for this type of behavior. With my excessive amount of energy, I couldn't sit still. I would not sit still long enough to finish my school homework or to do chores around the house. I could read from a very early age, but I just wanted to play with my friends, climb trees, play marbles, or do things kids do.

The incessant negativity and ridicule from family and friends, caused me to become suicidal. I admit that I attempted suicide a few times... To no avail, thankfully! When that did not work out, I decided to give myself a reason to live. I began to dream of a better life. Those dreams fueled my desire to live. I had things to do, people to help, and problems to solve.

I promised myself that I would become successful regardless what anyone said or thought about me. I became immune to negative suggestions or words, even when they said I wasn't smart enough, I talked too much, my head was too big, or I was too fat. I never allowed their words to get into my head. My family used to say I was a dreamer; to them, I daydreamed too much and should have taken my head out of the clouds to accept reality,

In my research and readings of other persons work who have spoken about the quest for fulfilling purpose the following is widely underscored:

Never accept someone else's reality as your own. Find your truth, your passion, what makes you happy, what gets you excited, find what makes you want to get up every day and have fun doing it for the rest of your life.

I remember when I was about 15 years old, I walked into a bank with a family member. As I walked into the bank, I immediately noticed a young man working behind a desk, he was well-dressed in a white shirt and blue tie, he looked polished and professional. I turned to the person I was with and said to them that I was going to work in a bank when I grew up. They replied by saying that the job I wanted was too good for me. That I should stick to manual labor because that's what I was good for. This response emotionally crushed me because the person that made the statement was someone I looked to for encouragement; they destroyed my heart with their words and didn't even know it. I decided right then and there that I would always believe in myself—even if one else did. I suddenly knew deep in my heart I was going to make it. It felt like a fire rose within me. I started telling my friends and anyone who would listen about what I would do when I grew up. I told them how I would travel to different countries, own my own business, marry a beautiful woman and have two or three children. I was going to make a difference! I dreamt with great detail about the lifestyle I would live, the people I would have around me, and the type of impact I would make on the world.

Visualization is a vital part of achieving your dreams. If you can see it, you can achieve it. I visualized every area of my life, down to its most minute details. I spent time in the spirit realm, in the area of the imagination, or as some call it the visualization zone, or what others call daydreaming.

I practiced visualization in every area of my life, until I felt it in the pit of my stomach. My life changed when I met JESUS. Although it didn't get better immediately, I felt an inexplicable sense of unconditional love. For the first time I was standing on a firm foundation, and I knew without any reservation, Christ, to be my firm foundation. Christ for me, became my guarantee that whatever life threw at me, I was going to make it. I remember the days I had no food to eat, He provided. I was homeless for a short time in my life, but God sent a Good Samaritan that saved me from freezing to death in the middle of winter. Even when I did wrong, Jesus was still there. He never gave up on me and as a result I never gave up hope.

As long as you stand (having done all you can) when its tough, because you don't know when you will hit your date with destiny. The day God will step in and change everything around you. Prayer or meditation is an excellent place to start transforming your surroundings. When you pray, ask God for creative ideas, a real insight into who you are, and ask for greater faith and revelation knowledge.

How did Noah know how to build an ark if he had never seen the rain? That was revelation knowledge. How could David stand before a giant with a sling shot and a few stones (Faith)? How did Shadrak, Meshack, and Abednego know that if they stood up for God, they would not be burned in the fiery furnace (Faith)? How did Daniel know if he was thrown in the lion's den, that he would not be eaten, (Faith)?

For every fight we will face in our lives we will need faith to achieve the victory we desire. The Bible says, if you have faith, like a grain of a mustard seed, you will say to the mountain in your life, 'Move from here to there,' and it will move, and nothing will be impossible for you.

Faith in God and revelation knowledge will bring you to another level of understanding that raises you above your situation. Armed with the correct information will help you to overcome anything that would come up against you.

Know that you know, that you know, the knowledge of who God is will help you face any circumstance just like Shadrach, Meshach, Abednego, and Daniel; they must have known God so much that when they were faced with death, they refused to lose their confidence in him.

One word I can give you that I can guarantee will change your life. One word that will move you from poor to rich, one word that can and will transform your life if you so choose. The word is DECISION. Do you remember the day you gave your life to Jesus Christ, your mom or some family member told you about Jesus, your friends, for some of you it was your co-worker, the guy you met at that supermarket or the person who you met in the parking lot? Still, Jesus makes a difference in our life's the day we decided to accept him as our Lord and Savior. The decision I made that day to accept Jesus as my Lord and savior forever changed my life.

The God of our Lord Jesus Christ, the father of glory, may give unto you the spirit of wisdom and revelation in the knowledge of him. -Ephesians 1:17

What do you desire? Can you tell the difference between being asleep or being awake? Here is how you might be able to know if you're sleeping or awake. You're still "asleep" if you are feeling unfulfilled in with your life, you think something is missing, or there is something you should be doing, and you're not doing it, you're still searching for purpose in your life, you're frustrated, and living with the regret about something in your past; a decision you shoulda, coulda, woulda, done differently. *WAKE-UP!* King Solomon provided us keen insight regarding this slumbering state of existence in Proverbs 6:9-11.

He Asked:
  1. How long will you lie there, you sluggard?
  2. When will you get up from your sleep?

He Answered:
> *A little sleep, a little slumber,*
>   *a little folding of the hands to rest*
> *and poverty will come on you like a bandit,*
>   *and scarcity like an armed man.*

Our life journey is a winding road ridden with potholes, bumps, hills, and valleys. At specific junctures, the road turns into steep hills or high mountains and even some pitfalls. The journey called life can at times appear quite scary or difficult, although occasionally, your predicaments are entirely fate's blunders; or per chance, they are your own. Your characteristics roughly resemble a steering wheel for your journey. They could be positive traits, which could steer you on a more decent path, or negative traits, which could guide you down a road that's, well, not so honorable. Although you have no control over fate, you have power over your own "personal choices" and could thus widen or narrow your chances of a smooth, prosperous journey. Also, it is essential to remember that you are not alone. I have met many others on this road called life with the same experiences as me, where others are navigating their journeys and floundering through their bumps or valleys. Finding others who share similar experiences could provide support and encouragement, thus making the trip of life more enjoyable. No matter what life throws at you, remember that you will pull through and be transformed for the better because of it.

I gave my life to Christ when I was a teenager. As a teenager, I had to deal with my share of peer pressure. It seems after I gave my life to the Lord, all kinds of temptations showed up. For a time, I resisted the enemy, but after a while, I fell right back into my sinful nature. I once had an individual lock me into a room with a girl who was older, because they wanted to trap me into giving them a grandchild. My friends started offering me marijuana to smoke; I am still saying no to this day. I started sneaking out of church to go to parties and clubs. My life was on a downward spiral.

It was at that point my mother noticed and decided to send me to Canada to live. I lived with a family member for a year and was thrown out of their house in the middle of winter with no money. But God stepped in that very same day. I circled the neighborhood contemplating what I would do since I had no where to go and no money on hand. I met an old man, he saw the look of sorrow on my face and asked me what was wrong. I proceeded to tell him what had just happened to me. After I finished telling him my story, he explained to me that he owned a rooming house, and he happened to have one room for rent. It would cost $75 per week. I told him I didn't have any money because I had used all the money I had to buy presents for my family—the same family who had just thrown me out of their home. He asked if I had a job, and I explained how I only had a part-time job because I was in college. My part-time job, at the time, was paying me $150 per week. He said if I wanted to move in, I would have to pay him $375. So we agreed that I would pay him $100 per week for four weeks. That meant after I paid him $100 per week I had just enough for my bus pass for a month and lunch for two days at school. So, instead of buying my regular lunch I bought two bottles of peanut butter and three loaves of bread. I ate bread, peanut butter, and water for breakfast, lunch, and dinner for one month and God kept me. I decided the night my family put me out that they would never see me suffer; they would never see me beg for bread. I prayed for God to give me the strength to stand by my promise, and he did. I graduated from college and went on to become successful. A decision I never regretted making.

I traced every fruitful decision I ever made in my life back to God. Knowing full well that the Holy Spirit is a part of me, guiding me, teaching me, and protecting me. Sometimes I would listen to Him, and other times not so much. I did not always listen to what the Holy Spirit advised me to do. Yet, for every mistake I made or wrong decision I gave into, He forgave me.

What have you built your life upon? One can make the mistake of building our lives on just our intellect, education, influential friends, the money we earn, or our good looks. But, all those things will and can fade away. Money might never run out, but it cannot buy you happiness; and our physical looks will fade. Friends and family might leave or forsake you, and they surely cannot give you total fulfillment. We are like the Samaritan woman (better known as the woman at the well), whether we want to admit it or not, we desire fulfillment in our lives.

Only Jesus can give us total fulfillment. In John 4:13-14, Jesus said **whosoever drinks of this water shall thirst again** (he is referring to things we can get in this world, thinking they will make us happy) **But whosoever drinks the water that I** (Jesus) **give him shall never thirst. Still, the water that I** (Jesus) **shall give him shall be in him a well of water springing up into everlasting life.** When we drink this water Jesus is referring too we will have all the money we need, the family, the friends, and influence because he will provide all our needs according to His riches in glory, but we have to put Him first.

*WE WILL NOT GET ALL GOD HAS FOR US
IF WE HAVE ONE FOOT IN CHRIST
AND THE OTHER OUT IN THE WORLD.*

I remember negotiating with God, saying it's okay to be involved in church and still go to the club. I wasn't doing anything wrong, and I have a glass of wine and occasionally remember you (God) turned the water into wine, so it must be okay to drink wine; in the club. I listened to some music, you said singing is good, and all they are playing here is love songs, and God is love. These were my rationalizing thoughts. I have friends who smoke marijuana and told me it was okay to smoke it because God made the trees and the weed.

However, Jesus said, **what does it profit a man to gain the world and lose his soul?** In order for my life to turn around, I had to make a conscious decision, either serve God by being 50% in the Christ and 50% in the world, in other words living a life that seemed right to me, or serve him 100% with no strings attached. I now serve him 150%.

When I turned twenty-five, I thought I was invincible and on top of the world. I was armed with a Bachelor of Science Degree in Business Administration. I worked for one of the top consulting firms in the world. On the side, I owned my own import/export company that was doing great; I had my sports car and my apartment, and everything was going right. I could do no wrong. Women were everywhere. I remember dating two or three women at one time and sleeping with them and their friends. I thought life was good. I felt like I was on top of the world. When everything is going well in your life, the enemy will make you believe you don't need God; you're doing well all by yourself, look at what you have achieved all by yourself.

11

In retrospect, I seemed to only remember God whenever I was in trouble, and only then did I need Him. Yet in all his faithfulness, and despite all my faults, He continued to love me and help me out.

One of the many lessons I learned early in life is that setbacks, discouragement, or negativity doesn't make you or break you. It's what we do with them that defines us. The things we say to ourselves when things come at us. Do we accept them or reject them? Always remember death and life are in the power of the tongue. The more you speak life-giving words to yourself, the stronger the fighter in you becomes. Because a *great fight is a product of great faith!*

CHAPTER 2

DESIGNING YOUR DESTINY

During the '70s, two songs became my anthems, the first was *Hold on to your Dreams* by William "Wee Gee" Howard, and the second was, *Greatest Love of All,* by George Benson. Those were my theme songs, they were my biggest inspiration growing up. There is a verse in the song *Hold on to your Dreams* that says: *"Mr. Sun should you fail to shine, dreams are the sunshine of the mind, dreams are the wings of the mind, you can fly anytime you like."*

What do you want out of life, and how are you going to get it? There are lots of Christians who don't like the word PROCESS; they want God to give them everything right now. However, the God we serve is a God of decency and order. This translates to, "God's Seasons are different from our timing."

Let's for a moment imagine your heart is a farm or a field, and your mind is its farmer; weeds and wheat are the plants to be sowed. You must be careful what you allow into your field of thoughts, so you must watch what you meditate on daily—for whatsoever you meditate on daily will grow in the field of your heart. This means that whatever type of thoughts you sow in your mind, is the type of harvest you reap in your life. The bible states, it's not what goes into a man that defiles him, rather it is what comes out of him (Matthew:15, v17-18). So what thoughts are governing you? Whatever you have in your life today is what you have let in and whatever the devil throws at you can always be shut out with God's word. Armed with God's word you can turn any situation around.

To fully grasp this, we must integrate it with another important concept. God works in seasons, not in time. As human beings, we want everything in fifteen seconds or less. If we're to get, from God, the result we desire, we must ask ourselves, is this the right season for it? If the answer is YES, you have to prepare the ground (Prepare your Heart). Plant the seed (the Word) every day you awake. Plant the Word and meditate on it. The word will grow in your life. The Word will process you. Words create an expectation of reality and what is promised. A farmer prepares the soil before he plants the seed; he doesn't just throw the seed on the ground and expect them to grow or produce. He has to till the ground, but first he decides what type of seeds to plant. A good farmer doesn't plant tomatoes when he knows he wants corn. He knows which food grows best in which season. You must be purposeful and specific about what you want from God. Don't ask God for a big house when you know you're unable to maintain it in your present state. Don't just ask God for a better job when you know you're not qualified for the position, you might have to further your education as a way to prepare yourself for the position you're asking God for. According to Ephesians 4:23, *Let the Spirit change your way of thinking.* The word of God inspires us to participate in the future that is promised. What do you believe in? Some people build their lives upon their achievements or upon who they may know, (their Rolodex of friends).

When I look back on my life, I can now see where the hand of God guided me. Even when I walked out of his will; He protected me and covered me with His love. The Holy Spirit later revealed to me some of the ways which God had guided my life which I was oblivious to.

From the age of four to Nineteen years of age, I built my life on the following two scriptures: Psalm 118:2, which is later repeated by Jesus in Mark 12: 10.

"The stone which the builder rejected becomes the head of the corner." -Psalm 118:2

I was raised in an environment where family members reinforced negative thoughts about me including the belief that I would not turn out to be anything good or that I was worthless. One day God sent a woman to turn all this around while I was still at the age of four, we called her Aunt Phil. Though she was not our biological Aunt, we called her that in respect. One day Aunt Phil overheard members of my family saying I would never amount to anything; because of the way they perceived me to be. She immediately began to rebuke them by saying she believed that when I was ready I would settle down and study my books, and do better than all my siblings and peers in knowledge and success. She recited, "the stone the builders refused shall be the head corner stone."

The act of her coming to my defense moved me to my core. Prior to her, no one ever defended me or stood up for me. Whenever Aunt Phil heard anyone say anything negative about any of the children in my neighborhood she stood up for them. This made her the most loved woman of all. Those of my generation who grew up in that area felt blessed to have known her.

From that day on, I decided to prove everyone wrong concerning the negative perceptions they held of me. From that day forward, the Bible verse Matthew 21:42 meant something deep to me. I memorized it and never let it go. Every time someone said something negative about me I instantly recited that verse.

Never underestimate the power of encouragement. We must never be too busy to say a kind word of encouragement to someone, even if you don't know that person. My great grandmother would always say *"Encouragement, sweetens labor."*

I was baptized as a teenager and studied the word of God enthusiastically. When I was about to leave my home in Jamaica, my mother, then a Christian herself and a strong prayer warrior, decided to have a prayer meeting for me the day before I left. In the middle of this prayer meeting the Holy Spirit took over and a prophecy was spoken over my life. At the end of the session, the lady who spoke the prophetic word stated that the Lord said I should read Psalm 27 and commit it to memory. When I got home, I read the scripture, but never took it seriously. Later while in Canada as a young man, at age twenty, the Lord brought the scripture back to me. At the time I was working very hard. I had broken my relationship with God and stepped out of his will. A series of events that followed immediately caused me to revisit this scripture and commit it to memory. It became my line of defense from then on. I learned that there was power in reading the scripture, committing it to memory, and living by it. Planting scripture in your heart enables it to grow and live in you, so that whenever you need God to show up for you. You can confidently call on Him, and remind Him of the promises in His Word (especially those given personally to you).

> *The LORD is my light and my salvation whom shall I fear?*
> *The LORD is the strength of my life of whom shall I be afraid?*
> *When the wicked, even mine enemies and my foes came upon me to eat my flesh they stumbled and fell. Though a host should encamp against me my heart shall not fear, though war should rise against me, in this will I be confident.*
> *One thing have I desired of the LORD that I will seek after that I may dwell in the house of the LORD all the days of my life to behold the beauty of the LORD and to inquire in His temple.*
> *For in the time of trouble He SHALL hide me in His pavilion in the secret of His tabernacle SHALL He hide me, he SHALL set me upon a rock and now shall mine head be lifted up above mine enemies round about me therefore will I offer in His tabernacle sacrifices of joy, I will sing yea I will sing praises unto the LORD.*
> *Hear O LORD when I cry with my voice have*

mercy also upon me and answer me. When thou saidth, seek ye my face my heart said unto thee, thy face LORD will I seek. Hide not thy face far from me put not thy servant away in anger, thou hast been my help leave me not neither forsake me O GOD of my salvation.

When my father and my mother forsake me, then the LORD will take me up. Teach me thy way O LORD and lead me in a plain path because of mine enemies. Deliver me not over unto the will of mine enemies for false witnesses are raised up against me and such as breathe out cruelty. I had fainted unless I had believed to see the goodness of the LORD in the land of the living. Wait on the LORD, be of good courage and he shall strengthen thine heart: wait I say on the LORD.

-Psalm 27

Negative thinking can be a habit of your mind. We have been told we *can't* so many times in our lives that we automatically default to that way of thinking—without even thinking! Often words remain in our minds because of intriguing story cadences; sometimes, those words aren't positive or kind, for example the old adage that says "sticks and stones might break my bones, but words will never hurt me." Words wound, words also heal, words edify, and words encourage. We may or may not gain strength from the stories we tell ourselves.

We all need encouragement to pursue a dream or move beyond our hurts or change negative patterns in our lives.

If you don't have an encourager in your life, look within the pages of scripture for wisdom and encouragement. Tune out negative words and focus on positive ones. You may want to consider the following scripture,

> *"Set a guard, O Lord, over my mouth;*
> *Keep watch over the door of my lips to keep me*
> *from speaking thoughtlessly." -Psalm 141:3*

CHAPTER 3

THE DANGER OF KNOWLEDGE

Allowing God to shape your life means you must learn to move in seasons. God moves in seasons, not in time. In other words, is the season you're in God's time? At the beginning of every year, most people jot down their resolutions or what they would like to accomplish for that year, but 2020 was an exception as it seemed the entire world came to a screeching halt with the outbreak of COVID-19.

In 1985, a friend of mine introduced me to one of the top motivational speakers in Canada. I spent the next two days at a conference absorbing everything this man had to say. Because of this teaching, I started to believe that if I just started speaking positive words in my life, everything I wanted I would have, all I had to do was believe!

So I began posting signs all over my apartment, positive words, and different types of charts. I even started chanting every night for two hours. I thought that all I had to do was think positive thoughts, and positive things would start happening. I started to believe that I didn't need God and that I could do everything myself. I told myself I was all powerful, and all knowing, because I was successful in corporate America. I was invited to sit on the board of directors for a large and successful corporation. I started my own business and was asked to represent certain corporations and non-profit organizations with governments in the Caribbean negotiating the merger and acquisition of large Government-owned corporations. I was successful, I was considered a self-made man. God had little or no part in my life or my successes. I did it all through positive thinking. This success went on for a few years and soon, my career was at the stage where it was ready for the next level, the big times, the place where we only talked about hundred million dollar deals. A place where your fee on one deal could range from ten million to one hundred million dollars. At this stage of my career, I went out and bought an offshore bank. My thinking was, I am about to make big money. I need to own a bank to put it in! But to my surprise, it seemed like one day I woke up, and without notice, everything started going wrong, everything started falling apart. I became frantic and started programming myself every day by telling myself that there was nothing happening that I couldn't fix, but as fast as I plugged one hole, another one would burst open. I continued speaking positive words in my life, and this went on for years. It eventually came to a stop when I lost everything. My business, marriage, investments, and money. As a result, even some of my friends stepped away from me, saying there must be a curse on me as it was impossible for a man to one day be at the top of his career and lose everything in another day without warning! They couldn't understand.

I remember my grandmother looking at me and asking what went wrong? She, too, found it hard to believe that I was at the top of the mountain one day, and the next thing she knew, I was scraping the bottom of the barrel. The giants in front of me seemed much larger than what was inside of me. Finally, God took charge to get my attention, and He allowed the enemy to strip everything from me. Suddenly, I found myself praying a lot and asking God for creative ideas on how to stop this avalanche in my life. You see, over the years, my relationship with God had become non-existent. I had stopped praying, and I never sought His will for my life. He was not a part of my master plan, and I thought I never needed Him. After all, I had a good education, was somewhat successful, and had powerful friends.

When this abrupt change entered into my life, I was not prepared for it. Don't get me wrong, I had a rainy day backup plan, a full-proof plan, or so I thought. But, as it turned out, I remained in my wilderness place for two and half years. I did not know if I was coming or going. It was in that place that the Holy Spirit started working on me. I began to redevelop my relationship with Christ. I had to learn to trust Him and believe that right where I stood, at that time of my life, was a place He could guide me to my promised land from.

Learn How to trust God when you're in the middle of a storm. We are humans, and all of us have been through a storm or two; none of us are immune to the storms of life; they are guaranteed to come. Storms come in many forms, like losing a job, developing health issues, or legal issues, dealing with financial struggles, or losing a loved one. Storms can happen on the job, in relationships, or even in ministry. Any area of life can bring stress, frustration, and emotional chaos at times.

When the storm comes or unexpectedly strikes, it leaves us feeling hurt, frustration, despair, and vulnerability. When a storm appears, we are tempted to ask ourselves questions like:

Why is this happening?
When will the pain stop!
Where is God in all this chaos?
What is the reason for this?

So what do we do when we're in the storm? I remember a Bible story about Peter, in when he walked on water in the midst of a storm; he started to sink, and he called out to Jesus. In return Jesus reached out to him.

When I was in the middle of my storm, I doubted God. I even asked Him in some way to prove himself. However, even when he showed up, my fear overrode my faith. Although faith is always the goal, our fear can sometimes win at the moment.

I believe principally we all know that when we cry out to God, He hears our prayers and is ready to help us. We read about the promises of Him being with us like in Joshua 1:9 which states, **"Be strong and courageous; do not be frightened or dismayed, for the Lord your God is with you wherever you go."** Also, we read in Psalm 145:18–19 that **"The Lord is near to all who call on him, to all who call on him in truth. He fulfills the desires of those who fear him; he hears their cry and saves them."** Although we are aware of these promises, how often do we allow our doubt to override our faith and trust in Him? A whole lot!

The minute I began building my faith and trust in Jesus Christ, I began overcoming my circumstances. My fight became great when my faith became greater. The Bible stresses, "God has already overcome the world!" John 16:33 explains, *"I have told you all this so that you may have peace in me. Here on Earth, you will have many trials and sorrows. But take heart, because I have overcome the world."* When we abide in and are saved by Him through grace, we are also overcomers. He promises that we will indeed have troubles, but that He has already overcome them all.

I had to learn to tap into God's power to overcome my difficult circumstances with His strength. The first thing I did to get my victory was to go back to the basics. I started by reading God's word. I had to remind myself of His promises that He would never leave or forsake me. To get the results I was looking for, I had to overcome my fears; the enemy wants us to fear the challenges that might come into our lives. Fear is not of God; we must learn how to fight fear and anxiety by focusing on God.

We must choose to trust. It's that simple. It is a choice we must make daily. Do you ever ask yourself why we go through storms? I have learned in my life's journey; there is a greater purpose in your trials—God may use it to help others. 1 Peter 5:10 says, *"And after you have suffered a little while, the God of all grace, who has called you to his eternal glory in Christ, will himself restore, confirm, strengthen, and establish you."*

What are you asking God to do in your life? Are you asking him to heal you, bless your business, bless and restore your family as well as lead you into your promised land?

Many people have found it difficult to operate in faith because they either don't know God's Word or they allow the word to get choked by the world's knowledge. Fear comes through a lack of understanding of God's word, just as faith comes through the knowing, believing, and experiencing of God's words. Most Christians today (even Spirit-filled Christians) are full of knowledge about operating in the world system. Still, they are deficient in the knowledge it takes to prosper in God's system. So, it is not really a faith problem that exists, but it is rather a Word problem. Our mind is similar to a computer. It acts upon the knowledge put into it. If all you have is basic knowledge, then all you can attain are basic results. But, we can reprogram ourselves and change our lives with the Word of God that will enable us to get phenomenal results. For this to happen, we must become open to knowledge. Just keep in mind you won't learn how to fly overnight. You will experience failures. You won't understand all the laws of faith instantly, and you may fall flat on your face a few times before you start seeing faith produce. But, the Law of faith, which created everything, is a million times more sure than the laws of gravity. God's knowledge and how faith works are not hidden from You, It's in the Word of God.

Pray Ephesians 1:15-23 with me, as a prayer to receive the knowledge of God. Believe that you receive, and watch faith begin producing in your life.

To integrate your faith into your everyday life, so it becomes a natural expression of who you are I encourage the following:

- Listen and obey: you must always be ready to learn.
- Open your ears for knowledge. Proverbs 18:15 states, *"An understanding mind gains knowledge; the ear of the wise seeks knowledge."*
- Be slow to speak
- Pray about it: ask God to give you complete knowledge of his will and give you spiritual wisdom and understanding.

- Avoid negativity, that means do everything without complaining and arguing so that no one can criticize you; stay away from negative people
- Share your faith in love. Love never gives up, never loses faith, is always hopeful, and endures through every circumstance. Trust God to work it out for you.

SPEAK INTO YOUR LIFE

Words are powerful. Words are descriptive. Words are creative; the bible says God spoke words, and the world was formed. In our society today words are being used as weapons, words are used to cause fear, hatred, and separation. We must make sure that when we use our weapon called words, we use it to uplift others.

Words turn into happiness
Words turn into peace
Words turn into money
Words turn into perfect health
Words change lives

> ***Death and life are in the power of the tongue***
> ***-Proverbs 18:21***

God's promises or positive words should not only make you feel good or excited, but give you power. There is power in the Word of God, and the principles of God will guide you to prosperity.

As Christians, if we believe in the promises of God, we should not have a problem speaking faith-filled words into our lives. The words of our mouth have control over our lives. What comes out of our mouth will determine our future. You must also know who's positive words you are speaking.

If you want to receive all you can from God, you must take time to study the Bible. Then, become open to receiving revelation knowledge.

Here are some steps you can take to hear from the Lord.

1. Read the scripture several times. Ask God to reveal the meaning of specific scriptures to you and listen for God to speak to you.

2. Be Thankful. To receive revelation knowledge, you must have a spirit of gratitude.

3. Work the Word. Putting the word you receive into action will allow you to be open to receive revelation knowledge. James 2:17 teaches us that faith doesn't work if it's dead.

Jesus showed us the power our words have in Mark 11:13-14 & 20, ***"And seeing a fig tree afar off having leaves, he (Jesus) came, if haply he might find anything thereon: and when he came to it, he found nothing but leaves; for the time of figs was not yet. And Jesus answered and said unto it, No man eat the fruit of thee hereafter forever. And his disciples heard it. And in the morning, as they passed by, they saw the fig tree dried up from the roots."***

Other examples of words bringing forth life can be found in John 11:43-44, ***And when he thus had spoken, he (Jesus) cried with a loud voice, Lazarus, come forth. And he that was dead came forth, bound hand and foot with grave clothes and his face was bound about with a napkin. Jesus said unto them, loose him, and let him go'"***

We can see from these two examples just how powerful our words can be. It is our privilege and responsibility as believers in Christ to speak forth positive life giving words in a world immersed in negativity. Proverbs 12:25 also reads, "Heaviness in the heart of man maketh it stoop: but a good word maketh it glad." and Proverbs 16:24 "pleasant words are as a honeycomb, sweet to the soul, and health to the bones." Discover what God's Word says about you and speak those words over your life.

Sometimes situations show up in the form of a challenge, like the challenge of Goliath and the fighting words in the story. David was offended by the comments of Goliath. However, the spirit of boldness came upon him, and even though he was a boy, he was offended to the point that he accepted the challenge to defend the honor of God and the Israelites.

FAITH AND SELF-CONFIDENCE

Faith without works is dead; in other words, work your faith. The word *work* is a verb. If you have faith for something, you not only believe it, the energy of that belief sends a feeling of excitement throughout your body. If your banker calls you one morning and tells you that after reviewing your account, they found an error and want you to know they are going to wipe out all your debt, for some of us, we would be excited, and we would be doing cartwheels, screaming and yelling at the top of our lungs.

One of the reasons for my success is having faith in God and/or confidence in myself. Yet, having confidence in yourself is not as easy as it sounds. I talk to a lot of people, many of whom have shared with me that the reason they have not manifested what they desire from life is due to lack of faith in themselves and/or lack of faith in God's ability to help them overcome obstacles.

What does it mean to have confidence in yourself? Self confidence is a personal characteristic. Having self-confidence is a good thing. A strong sense of confidence and self-esteem allows people to go out in the world and reach their goals. Faith toward God and our unwavering confidence in our relationship with Him. When we have faith in God, we are confident that He is not only able but willing—even eager—to do what we ask of Him because of the special place we have in His heart. I think it is important to note that our faith should be in God and not in our own. Having faith in God's promises allows us to find fulfillment in life. You must have confidence in yourself that you can do what He has called you to do. If you're going to achieve your dream you will need to develop the confidence to follow your dreams while knowing that He will give you the desires of your heart.

Do self examinations, take a step back and look at yourself, take inventory of your strengths and weaknesses. By analyzing your strengths and weaknesses you can realize how far you have come. At that point, start being proud of your achievements; if you're a good listener be proud of that, if you're a great organizer be proud of that, if you serve in your church or community be proud of that. Being proud of your strengths will help you to build self confidence and self-confidence is CRUCIAL for any kind of success.

> ***Being confident of this, that he who began a good work in you will carry it on to completion until the day of Christ Jesus***
> ***-Philippians 1:6***

WHAT DOES CONFIDENCE HAVE TO DO WITH FAITH?

Unlock the Power of Self-Confidence

Vision – Develop a big vision; make sure your purpose is being fulfilled in your vision. Your purpose should bring you joy.

Commitment – Commit to your goal. Create the habit of doing at least one thing daily that will move you towards achieving your goal.

Knowledge – Wisdom is the principal thing, Mike Murdock said every problem is a wisdom problem there is no problem that doesn't have a biblical solution.

Never give up - Hard work will pay off.

Know What You Want - know exactly what you want to achieve. Without a vision the people perish.

Have faith – always think positive, live a life of great expectation, always smile.

Pray or meditate daily – knowing that your faith rests in God, by praying you will improve your self-confidence . Say a silent prayer.

> *So do not throw away your confidence; it will be richly rewarded. You need to persevere so that when you have done the will of God, you will receive what he has promised.*
> *Hebrews 10:35-36 (NIV)*

CHAPTER 4

MASTERING THE ART OF MANIFESTATION

The everyday story of life, love, and death is what connects us all as human beings. Whether we know it or not, like it or not, our lives are our own choice. In this society, we are all expecting (rightly or wrongly) to give our lives purpose and meaning by using our skills and resources, even while we, at times, lack the internal tools and materials needed for the artists within us to be conceived and executed.

As it relates to our spiritual life—once you invite the Holy Spirit in, He starts to create the masterpiece.

The word says: *"Seek ye first the kingdom of God and His righteousness and all things will be added to you"*, but we can block the blessing because of what we allow to enter our spiritual life; things like hatred, jealousy, disobedience, envy, and strife. These type of seeds will block the evidence of blessings in your life.

God says you're blessed, but the proof will never show

up if there is strife. If you have hatred in your heart, you're blocking love. if you have anger against your fellow man and not forgiveness, you are also blocking the blessing of love in your life. If you have the spirit of disobedience, then there is a chance you're blocking your bountiful blessings.

Some believers want to use God like a magician. They show up to church on Sunday wanting him to magically fix their problems, but continue living throughout the week outside of His will and expect God to understand. There is no time in their lives to spend time with Him each day in prayer, they only open their bible on a Sunday if they show up for church. Some people believe that should be enough for God. We need to spend time planting the word in our heart (in good ground) so we can reap the harvest He promises us.

Everyone wants to own a home, but not everyone wants to go through the loan process of homeownership. In every area of our lives we have to go through a process in order to get somewhere or to achieve something. It's the same way with our Christian walk, every prophet, great leader, every patriarch, every lesson taught in the bible, each has something to do with processing. Allowing God to mold and reshape us to what He has called us to be. God is interested in our end product. As a Christian, if we want to get anything from God, we have to be willing to allow Him to process us.

PROCESS OF MANIFESTATION

Your thoughts originate from the "files of information" you have in the storage cabinets of your mind. So, where does this information come from? It comes from your past programming. Every single thought we have relates to life or how we feel about what we deserve. The holy spirit will help you create a strong feeling about your dreams, and the feeling will help you create the future you dream about. Our beliefs lead to our thoughts; our thoughts lead to our feelings; our feelings lead to our actions; our actions lead to our results.

This is the process of manifestation:

1. How strong is your passion to do what God has called you to do? Whenever you come to the awareness that God has a purpose for your life, you must take certain steps if you want the blessing of God to show up or if you want to fulfill purpose.

> *In the same way, faith by itself,*
> *if it is not accompanied by action, is dead.*
> *James 2:17*

2. Action means work, faith without works is dead. So, work your faith. You must have a desire for whatever you're doing. Desire is the fuel that will drive your purpose. If you have a weak desire you will apply weak effort. Strong work ethics with a strong desire will push you to fulfill your purpose. Another word for desire is passion.

3. You must have a straightforward and direct plan as to how you're going to accomplish your goal or your purpose. Ask God to help you fulfill His plan or purpose for your life. Remember in 1 Chronicle 28, when God told David to build a temple, God gave him the plans, the drawing, and the designs. David's desire was to build God's temple, but God told him although I am giving you the plan, I don't want you to build it. Your plan must be so clear that someone else can come along, pick it up, and complete it. David's plans were so clear that Solomon, his son, could take the plan God gave his father and complete it. Whenever God impregnates you with a purpose or gives you an assignment it's always for someone else, it is always designed to fulfill a need in someone else's life. I Chronicles 28

4. You must know why you're doing what you're going to do, its okay if your purpose provides you with financial success or because you're doing what God has call you to do you are now able to live in a mansion, drive an expensive car, go on exotic vacations with your family, even send your kids to private schools or buy that really expensive diamond ring you always wanted to buy your wife. You may even get that Rolex watch for your husband. Proverbs 18:16 reads, "A man's gift makes room for him, and brings him before great men." God has placed a gift or talent in every person that the world will make room for. Money is a great thing to have as long as it's in your hand and not in your heart.

5. Believe in your purpose. If God gives you a glimpse of your future and because the future God shows you looks too amazing to be realized you begin to doubt the possibility of it being achieved, you begin to speak of failure. Remember God said in Jeremiah 29:11, "For I know the thoughts that I think toward you, says the LORD, thoughts of peace and not of evil, to give you a future and a hope".

6. Be committed to God's plan for your life, totally committed to your purpose, meaning you must be willing to give 100%, never quit, never stop, never give up, be totally willing to go over any obstacles. Speak words of faith into your life.

When you are 100% committed to reaching your goals, you move from hoping to knowing you can do it, and you won't quit.

MOTIVATION

Challenges and difficulties are a part of life, and words of encouragement can often help you get out of a rut. It's easy to tell someone to hang in there and to keep a positive outlook when they are going through tough times, but when it happens to you, keeping your chin up isn't always the easiest thing to do. Even so, it's not impossible. There are a lot of things you can do to help yourself bounce- back and move forward. Whether you've been dealt a setback while working toward your goal, lost a loved one due to the pandemic, or feeling down and hopeless; inspirational words of encouragement can help.

What motivates you? Words can have a powerful impact on your mindset. Words do affect how we feel, and your feeling dictates your response. Make sure whatever motivates you comes from within. Some people use their personal experience of their lives to motivate themselves; because my family told me I wasn't going to come out to be anything, I used that as one of my motivations to prove them wrong, at the same time pushing to achieve my desires while doing the things I enjoy.

Most successful people use their bad experiences or failure as motivation to achieve instead of as a crutch. Motivation is like fuel in a plan; your dream will not take off if you're not motivated. There is enough time in everyone's days to work on your dream. There is no such thing as a lack of time, just a lack of motivation. You must become a positive thinker and speak positive at all times. Your words shape your world.

> *Finally, brothers, whatever is true, whatever is honorable, whatever is just, whatever is pure, whatever is lovely, whatever is commendable, if there is any excellence, if there is anything worthy of praise, think about these things. -Philippians 4:8*

It would help if you learned to be self-motivated. They say the law of Attraction includes the law of gratitude. One thing I practice every day is the law of gratitude. You must be grateful for where you are and where God has brought you from, and where you are at that time. Are you grateful for what you have in your life? Gratitude attracts abundance, and gratitude attracts peace of mind. Each day remember to show gratitude for even the smallest blessing.

Do you know that the Law of Attraction includes the Law of Gratitude? The Law of Attraction states that like attracts like. When you're grateful for what you already have, you will naturally attract more you can be thankful for. People who lack gratitude always find themselves living in poverty or not having the lifestyle they truly desire. They look upon themselves as lower than everyone else and wonder why they can't be better than what they are. It's' called self-guilt.

Never wait for someone to come along and pat you on the back and say well done that might never happen, because no one understands your purpose better than you do. Some of us want to be a millionaire, more money only allows you to pay off bills, but it can't buy good health or happiness. Learn to enjoy your journey, celebrate your success daily, show appreciation and express gratitude daily.

Ever wonder why when you look at rich people, you notice their prosperity or their riches, but never see the mountain of debt they have. Most rich persons I know are filled with gratitude. If you ask them how they got rich the first thing they will say is "I got lucky" they never credit their excellent education or their hard work. Wealthy people are filled with gratitude. Without gratitude, you have no power since the two connect together.

The relationship we have with God's word will affect how we react to the storms and disappointments in our lives. In trials, our thinking can lead to fear and deep depression or lead us to joyfully praising the Lord. We have to make a practice of renewing our minds with the word in order to stay strong in our faith. In my life, I've had trials that could have led me into despair however, as I made a practice of renewing my mind with the word of God, those same trials that once led me to despair now leads me to praising the Lord. "Your attitude, not your aptitude, will determine your altitude."

"A joyful heart is good medicine,
but a crushed spirit dries up the bones."
-Proverbs 17:22

"A joyful heart makes a cheerful countenance,
but sorrow of the heart crushes the spirit."
-Proverbs 15:13

"Although no one can go back and make a brand new start, anyone can start from now and make a brand new ending." – Carl Bard

Give thanks in all circumstances,
for this is God's will for you in Christ Jesus.
-1 Thessalonians 5:18

You must ask yourself these five questions before you embark on any project:

Why am I doing it?
What is the plan?
Do I believe in the vision or the project?
Am I willing to commit to the vision?

What's my passion or what is my desire for doing it? If your passion for doing it is self-centered don't do it, your purpose for doing it should be centered around one thing "what problem am I hoping to solve?" The answer can be cancer, homelessness, hunger, educational deficiencies, people who need legal or medical help or anything area where you feel to make a difference.

Your passion should move you to action, if you don't feel strongly about your purpose or your dreams, you will never accomplish it.

CHAPTER 5

HEROES ARE MADE FROM FIERY BATTLES

What matters most on your journey of life is how well you walk through the fire. It's easy to be happy when everything in life is going well. It's easy to love when your heart is not broken or hurting. It's easy to be generous when blessings are abundant. It's easy to feel like the risk was worth it when so far it's paying off.

But what about when everything starts going haywire? We can't control the things that happen to us, but we can control the way we react to them. Sometimes these are the experiences that define who we are or how we will live our lives.

How well do you live your life on your worst days? Sometimes a proverbial fire can bring the best out of us just like a diamond.

We can also use fire to cook food and that same fire, if not controlled, will burn down your house. Fire can also provide a light and show us the path through the darkness.

If you are walking through a fire of your own however big or small, this might be an excellent time to rewrite your future. Never allow the phrase "Hurt people, hurt people," to be the motto you live by. Treat people around you with dignity and love, regardless of whether or not they reciprocate the same. Exercising releases stress, take care of yourself. You can find some joy even in the darkest hours.

Find ways of forgiveness, for the people who need it most including yourself. Forgive even the ones that don't deserve it, so you can set yourself free.

Again, list the things you are grateful for, even when small graces are few and far between. Walk through the fire with your head held high and arms outstretched to others who might be dusting off the ash of their own battle fires.

I have made lots of mistakes in my life and failed many times, but the emotions I have about my life inspired me to never give up and keep on fighting.

Every millionaire biography I have ever read, whether it's Warren Buffet, Lee Iacocca, Bill Gates, Ted Turner, A.L. Williams and Tony Robbins etc., have all used the hurt in their life to motivate them to their greatest success in life.

Develop a passion for whatever you want out of life, see yourself successful every day, take ten minutes every day and find a quiet place and meditate or focus your thoughts on your dreams.

"Brethren, whatsoever things are true, whatsoever things are honest, whatsoever things are just, whatsoever things are pure, whatsoever things are lovely, whatsoever things are of good report; if there be any virtue, and if there be any praise, think on these things." -Philippians 4:8

One lesson I have learned as I got older is that some rules are made to be broken. For example, like when people say "Seeing you're black you can't amount to anything" or ``Be bold enough to live life on your terms, and never, ever apologize for it". "Go against the grain, refuse to conform, take the road less traveled instead of the well-beaten path." "Laugh in the face of adversity, and leap before you look and put God first in everything."

Every day you must speak positive words into your life; there is life and death in the tongue, so you must tell yourself that you will make it, and whatsoever God has birth in you shall come to pass.

> ***Death and life are in the power of the tongue:***
> ***and they that love it shall eat the fruit thereof.***
> ***Proverbs 18:21 NIV***

Develop an attitude of agreeing with what the Bible says, when you pray, believe it has been done, and It shall be done. Whatever you want from God you must possess it first in faith. Never doubt, if you believe that God is the supplier of your needs, then he will supply your needs. There is nothing impossible for God, and you must believe that whatsoever you ask for, you will receive. If you believe you will receive great things from God then have an attitude of excitement. If you woke up one morning and found out you won ten million dollars, your attitude, your energy, your very spirit would display excitement through and through, because you hold in your hand the winning ticket. Knowing some of us, we would call our bosses and tell them to take his job and shove it... before we even pick up the money. We would be thinking about all the things we are going to buy before we think about paying off our debts. The bible is our winning ticket, the promises of God is our guarantee that we are winners, we are the seed of Abraham, joint heirs with Christ.

There are seven promises God made to Abraham that we are entitled to, God said:

I will make you into a great nation.
I will bless you.
I will make your name great.
You will be a blessing.
I (God) will bless those who bless you.
I (God) will curse those who curse you.
All the people on earth will be blessed through you.

If you believe that you can have whatsoever your heart desires, then act like it, and start preparing yourself to receive it. When you pray, believe it has been done and it shall be done, if you believe you're going to receive something great your thoughts about that thing should be ecstatic. When your attitude shifts you start feeling excited in your spirit because you believe in your heart that it is going to happen. For those of us that are believers, I can never understand how we can believe with all our heart that our God has the power to save us from hell when we die, but he can't make our dreams come through or supply all our needs on earth. Things are going to happen in life, you're going to have obstacles and sometimes setbacks, but you must be purposeful about what you want out of life and NEVER lose faith.

Faith does not prevent life from happening. You cannot

say because you have faith negative things will not happen to you, but faith will carry you through life! Faith declares, "I will overcome!", "I will get through" or "I will be the man or the woman God has called me to be."

Sometimes we become overly concerned about people and what they will say. How will our friends feel? How will they respond? We then lose focus of our goals. It is important to get delivered from people's opinions and to be purposeful about accomplishing our goals. Faith is the only thing that will make our dreams come true. "Faith in God," makes sure your spirit is lined up with your purpose. In other words, make sure you believe in your heart that whatever you're working towards is exactly what you desire, it is what God wants for your life's purpose.

You will encounter obstacles. You will make mistakes. Be grateful for both. Your obstacles and mistakes will be your greatest teachers. And the only way to not make mistakes in this life is to do nothing, which is the biggest mistake of all.

Visualize your GOALS. The starting point of all achievement is desire. Keep this constantly in mind.

> *"Weak desires bring weak results, just as a small amount of fire makes a small amount of heat."-Napoleon Hill*

If you can't visualize yourself living your dream, you will never achieve it, Jesus said ***"What things soever you desire, when you pray, believe that you receive them, and ye shall have them". Mark 11:24 (KJV)***

Belief is a verb, whenever you believe in something your

believing should excite you. If you believe something good is going to happen you start feeling excited. If you believe that something bad is going to happen you start feeling sad even before the thing happens because you believe.

When it comes to your goal, your dream or your desire you must get excited. Lee Iacocca said, "The greatest discovery of my generation is that human beings can alter their lives by altering their attitudes of mind."

How would you feel if you accomplished your greatest desire, walked out your biggest dream? If you can't picture (see) yourself living your dream and experience the feeling of excitement about what you're seeing you will never accomplish your goal. Feeling your dream is very important. The power of positive thinking will never work if you don't have it. Desire is a feeling, believing is a verb.

ACTIVITY:

See your dream and feel yourself living your dreams. In other words, how would you feel if you woke up one day and found out someone wired Ten million dollars ($10,000,000) into your bank account ? You thought it was a mistake and so you go to your bank and say to the teller I think you made a mistake and put ten million dollars in my account. The bank manager came over to you and said no sir or no madam it is not a mistake someone wired the money to you. I bet your feelings would change for the rest of your life.

Begin by writing down your goals, your dreams, your desires and make a commitment to go after them. Lee Lacocca said, "The discipline of writing something down is the first step toward making it happen." Create measurable goals, don't create impossible ones. If you want to live in a million dollar home and you know that your present job can't maintain a million dollar home, set a measurable goal, don't lose sight of the million dollar home, but ask God to give you creative ideas so you can move your present position to the place where you can afford the million dollar home.

VISION IS VITAL

Vision is vital to live a fulfilled life, for those of us that grew up in church we remember this bible verse well, "where there is no vision the people perish." After Disney World in Orlando, Florida was finished, a reporter interviewed Michael Vance, the creative director at Disney, and proposed, "it's too bad Walt Disney did not live to see all of it. Mr. Vance responded by saying Walt did see it and that is precisely why we are seeing it today.

> *Build a man a fire, and he'll be warm for a day.*
> *Set a man on fire, and he'll be warm for the rest*
> *of his life. -Terry Pratchett*

If you want to experience how it feels to have faith that will prepare you to fight the giants in your life, you must get rid of F.E.A. R. (False Evidence Appearing Real). The false evidence we are talking about is the negative people in our lives that will transfer their negative words or reinforce the negativity we tell ourselves. Sometimes life will hit you in the head with a brick. Don't lose faith. We must learn to Face Everything and Respond (F.E.A.R). Open your eyes; look within. Are you satisfied with the life you're living?

The Great fight is a product of Great Faith, work hard for what you want because it won't come to you without a fight.

You have to stay strong, and become courageous, knowing that you can do anything you put your mind to. If somebody puts you down or criticizes you, keep believing in yourself and turn it into something positive.

In a battle, every hero needs a sword; the unique thing about a sword is the more you temper a sword, the stronger it becomes; the more you speak the words of God and believe in them, the more confident you will become. The more confidence or evidence you have that the word works will help you defend yourself in your time of need, meaning that you will act out of faith in the word of God rather than fear of the giant standing in front of you.

What are Giants? Giants are difficulties, people, or experiences in our lives, ie.,family or marriage problems, financial burdens, health issues, loss, depression, and much more.

Here is a list of giants some of us deal with daily:

1. Fear
2. Depression.
3 Anxiety.
4. Loneliness.
5. Mental illness.
6. Death of a spouse or family member.
7. Loss of a job or income; facing unemployment.
8. A sudden illness; harsh diagnosis.
9. Relationship issues, divorce, marital problems.
10. Addiction: drugs, alcohol, pornography, food, too much of any one thing.

In order for us to have victory over our Giants we must "Remember the victories of the past." David remembered:

God had given him strength to wrestle a lion and strong-arm a bear. Wouldn't He do the same with this giant? God will never let you fight giants, until you have proven to be FAITHFUL in the little things of your life. When you trust God with your PROBLEMS they will become POSSIBILITIES for God to work in your life.

There are financial giants. There are health giants. There are giants in your marriage, on your job, in your business, in your relationship with your kids. There are even giants in our ministry; for some of us there are even giant plants in our way blocking us from fulfilling our purpose. Giants of procrastination, giants of lack. In order for some of us to overcome our Giants, we might have to go back to school. For others to overcome health giants, they might have to start exercising and eating healthier.

It helps if you discover what you have to do to defeat the giants in your life. The first gift the holy spirit gave the disciples was the gift of courage. We must have courage to defeat our Giants, and courage only comes from trusting God's word which says *"I can do ALL things through Christ who strengthens me,"* Philippians 4:13.

CHAPTER 6

PROVEN STRATEGIES FOR SUCCESS

"They who have conquered doubt and fear have conquered failure"-James Allen

How do we define success, happiness, and a life well-lived for ourselves? This might seem obvious. But it isn't. Too often, we all form an idea of success that goes along with the consensus rather than one based off of our own criteria. Why? Because we don't clearly define what our criteria or our standards are.

We might say we want to be as rich as Elon Musk or as talented as Oprah Winfrey. Maybe we want to be as smart as Einstein, or as fast as Usain Bolt. Yet, the reality is that we tend to highlight and choose others' criteria to build our ideas of success and happiness around. We will sometimes choose the wealthiest person to define success. We also tell ourselves if we had a certain amount of money we would be a success. We sometimes choose the most athletic looking person to frame our ideas about fitness, but all of those people have many other characteristics, so we shouldn't just choose the one they leveraged the most to define success for ourselves.

We also can't just look at an example of someone we think meets our criteria and model them.

We should ask ourselves. What would make *you* successful in *your* mind? What would make *you* happy in life? At the end of your life, how would *you* know that *you* lived *your* life to the fullest?

Success is built upon the foundation of courage, hard work, and individual responsibility. Despite what others would have you believe, success is not built on resentment and fears.

To create a successful mindset, we must identify what our purpose is; what our strengths and weaknesses are. There is a quote that said "Choose a job you love, and you will never have to work a day in your life." I say find your purpose and live the rest of your life fulfilling it. Only what you do for God will last. An easy way to find your purpose is to ask some people who genuinely know you, to help you decide what your purpose should be based on and listen carefully to what their answer is. From their responses, you should begin to get a glimpse of what you would be good at. I have a friend that works at a title company. She truly did not like her job, she didn't like her boss, she didn't get along very well with her co-worker, she wanted to quit, but did not know what she wanted to do. After spending a weekend with a group of friends, listening to their problems and giving them advice, one of the girl casually said to her, "you're are a great listener, thanks for the great advice you gave me about my relationship."

Something clicked in her, she remembered as a child she

told herself she wanted to help people with their problems, she truly loved to listen to people and help them with their problem, she started think what it would be like being a counselor, she was so excited because she suddenly found something she truly loved, after going back home she immediately enrolled in evening class and started going after her dream.

What is God calling you to do?
How are you going to live the next ten years of your life?
What's important to you?
What action can you take right now that would move you towards your goal?

Picture yourself ten years from now and ask yourself, **"if I keep on the path I am presently on right now what will my life look like?"** and be honest with yourself, then ask yourself what would my life look like if I went after my dream or my hearts desires? What would I look like if I had a lot more money, a successful business, a healthy marriage, lose 20lbs, drive a better car, live in a bigger house, make my wife happy, make my husband happy or whatever is important to you right now, maybe it's finding the man of your dreams or the woman of your dreams, what decision will you make right now to make it happen?

"It's your moment of decision that your destiny is shaping, making a true decision means committing to achieving a result, and then cutting yourself off from any other possibility."-Anthony Robbins

To successfully direct our lives, we need to clarify and articulate our personal definitions of a well-lived life and we need to examine our values based upon our findings. Decide what we want to become in this lifetime. As much as possible, we need to eliminate the things that are truly impeding our growth in that direction.

***Blessed is the man who finds wisdom, the man who gains understanding. Happy is the man that finds wisdom, and the man that get understanding.
Proverbs 3: 13***

***For the merchandise of it is better than the merchandise of silver and
the gain thereof than fine gold.
-Proverbs 3:14***

Your gift will make room for you; your desire, and your purpose will provide for you—God has impregnated you with something that you can use to take care of your family.

5 KEYS TO WEALTH
"God gives us the POWER to gain Wealth."

There are five **POWER** keys to achieving wealth:

P – Plan. You must have a plan, what's your desire, what is your brand or your product? Give one word that defines who you are, you must have a clear goal; without a vision, the people perish. Suppose you're a person who loves to sell, find a product or service and use your gifts in that area. If I said Bill Gates, everyone would think Microsoft computer; if I say

Michael Jordan, everyone would say basketball. If I said Tiger Woods, everyone would say Golf. What would your friends or family say that defines you?

O – Organize. Assemble a team of people who believe in you and your dream, people who want to see your success and are willing to help you get there. Create a vision /dream board and put pictures of all the things you want in your life. If you want a luxury car, find one you love and put a picture of it on your dream board. If the following represent your desires add them : A Million dollar home, generous vacation, money in your bank account, find photos of all these things and place them on your dream board, and put the board in a place where you can see it every day.

W – Work. Work your plan and plan your work. every day, you must do something that will move you towards your goal. Make sure prayer is a part of your plan or plan a time every day to spend time praying for your purposes. *The Secret of your Future is hidden in your Daily Routine. When your heart decides the destination, your mind will design the map to reach it.-Mike Murdock*

E – Emotion. Feel the enthusiasm and excitement – you must get up every day excited about reaching your goal; use negative emotion to empower you. All the people in my life that told me I could not do it, I took those negative words, turned them around, and said to myself YES I CAN. Only keep people around you who will motivate you and encourage you. Say, "NO" negative people!

R – Results/Reward. – Set timelines for example, you should have a six-month goal, a one-year goal and a five-year goal; you should write out what your desires are or what you'll like to achieve in ten years and don't hold back. Never give up and be purposeful in your work be ready to learn new things.

6 Questions you should ask yourself to discover purpose:

1. What excites you – what's the one thing you would love to do for the rest of your life?
2. What are you naturally good at?
3. What do people typically ask you for help in?
4. If you had to teach something, what would you teach?
5. Who do I want to help –
what problem do I want to solve?
6. What would you regret not fully doing, being
or having in your life?

Once you've identified your purpose or mission in life, the next step is to turn that purpose into purposeful goals, start taking action. Find a place where your genius comes alive!

And the LORD answered me, and said, write the vision, and make it plain upon tables, that he may run that read it. -Habakkuk 2:2 -

WRITE OUT YOUR LIFE TIME DREAMS OR GOALS.
(Don't hold back)

Think of all the things you would want in your life, if you have these things right now (today) would you be happy?

You can't tithe your way to a blessing. Tithing is your reasonable service. A seed is anything you invest yourself in that improves your life or the life of others around you.

Brethren, I count not myself to have apprehended: but this one thing I do, forgetting those things which are behind, and reaching forth unto those things which are before, I press toward the mark for the prize of the high calling of God in Christ Jesus. -Philippians 3: 13-14

LIST ONE GOAL YOU WANT TO ACHIEVE IN YOUR LIFE:
Which one goal or desire do you have that if you fulfill this one desire in your lifetime you would be happy?

Ask, and it shall be given you; seek, and ye shall find; knock, and it shall be opened unto you. -Matthew 7:7

LIST YOUR ONE YEAR GOAL
List five things you would like to achieve in the next 12 months that would move you towards your goal.

LIST YOUR SIX MONTH GOAL

List one thing you would like to do in the next six months that would move you towards fulfilling the dream, your desire.

DAILY AGENDA

Your daily agenda is a written list of things you want to accomplish these things must be directly connected to your goal.

Evaluate your goal every time you reach your set time line.

Success Secret
(V+F)+A/W=R
(Vision + Faith) + Action/Work = Results

CHAPTER 7

BUILD YOUR DREAM BOARD

Let's recap! A great fight is a product of great faith, and without a vision, the people perish. Great triumphs can only come out of great trials! If you think vision boards are bogus, then the joke's on you! They work, and there's a straightforward explanation of why they work so well.

Creating a sacred space that displays what you want, will subconsciously and inspirationally help you focus and create a plan that brings your vision to life. What we focus on expands. When you start a Dream Board and place it in a space where you see it often, you essentially end up doing short visualization exercises throughout the day.

The purpose of using a dream board is to help you focus and create what you desire in life. It is something that almost all millionaires use. Your vision board should have pictures of the things you would like to have in your life, these pictures should inspire you to action, they should excite you to fulfill purpose.

Hang your DREAM board in a place you will look every day. You should look at this board daily, look at the picture you selected and start to think how you would feel if you have all the things on your vision board in your life right now, at this very moment.

SEE IT * BELIEVE IT * RECEIVE IT
See yourself having your heart's desire, believe that you deserve it and see yourself receiving it, imagine someone giving it to you.

3 STEPS FOR ANSWERED PRAYER

Step 1. ASK and it shall be given, ask God for what you want out of life, see yourself with the thing you desire.

Step 2. Believe for your Answer: believe with all your heart that God will answer your prayer (Have Faith).

Step 3. Receive: by faith you will receive whatsoever you are praying for.

> *"and whatever things you ask in prayer, believing, you will receive."*
> *-Matthew 21:22*

PROTECT YOUR DREAM

Don't tell everyone your dream or desire; if you know God gave you an idea or a passion for something, protect it. When my wife became pregnant with our first child, I became an overprotective husband because I knew the value of the blessing/gift my wife was carrying inside her stomach. For the first three months we told no one I made sure she ate right and took her vitamins. I made sure the seed she was carrying was growing healthy and was cared for. When God impregnates you with an idea you need to protect it. I have a friend that came up with a great idea. He was so excited he began to tell everyone he knew, after a while negative people got wind of the idea and started tell him he couldn't develop his idea. They spoke so many negative words into his life that he started to believe them and eventually gave up on the idea. You must guard your dream, and water it with prayer. Be discreet about the idea until you finish developing it. Don't allow anyone to distract you from your dream––refuse to quit! The secret to winning is your refusal to quit.

Joseph was seventeen years old, when one night he dreamed about shocks of wheat all bowing to one particular shock. When he shared this dream with his brothers, they said to him, are you going to reign over us? Or are you going to rule over us?" They hated him even more, and they were jealous because they knew he was their father's favorite. One day their father Jacob sent Joseph to see how his brothers and their flocks were doing. When they saw Joseph approaching from a distance, they looked at one another and said, "Hey, here comes the dreamer." They began to plot to kill him. They decided that if they killed him, they would kill his dream. We call those people dream killers. Get rid of them from around you. Never give up! Many of you feel trapped in failure, sickness, depression, distress and lack .Begin to dream in line with God's word, you must see yourself as a success. You are more than a conqueror, you must see yourself greater than your situation around you. "Greater is He that is in you than he that is in the world"

Thomas Edison failed over ten thousand times before he found the solution for the electric light he said; "I am not discouraged because every wrong attempt discarded is another step forward."

The electric light was a dream of Thomas Edison no matter how many times his experiment failed, he never gave up because of his dream. That's why we enjoy the advantages of the electric light today. Take small steps every day towards your goal; winners are people who are willing to move towards their goals one step at a time,

> ***A journey of a thousand miles begins with a single step -Lau Tzu***
>
> ***Dare to believe in your dream!***
> ***I've missed more than 9000 shots in my career. I've lost almost 300 games. 26 times, I've been trusted to take the game-winning shot and missed. I've failed over and over and over again in my life. And that is why I succeed.***
> ***-Michael Jordan***

Listen to the *still* voice. Trust your instincts. One day some friends of mine told me about a party that was happening in a rough part of town. Our favorite DJ was playing the music at the party. We all decided that we were going to attend the party. The problem I had was the party was being held on a Friday night, the same night I always go to youth fellowship at my church. I was excited all week about the party, Friday came, I asked my mother if I could go to church, she said yes; I left my home around 7 PM. As I got to my gate, I took my bible and hid it under a rock and turned to the opposite direction from my church. On my way to the party that was about five miles from my home, (about half-way) I heard an inner voice say turn around. Without hesitation, or a second thought I turned around and went the opposite direction towards the city to go hang out with some of my other friends. About an hour after I reached the city, I saw an ambulance and police cars with sirens on and flashing lights speed by my friends and I. They were heading toward the direction of the party. I had no knowledge of what had occurred. The next morning, I heard that at the party I was planning to attend there were men with guns who killed eight persons. This story stuck with me because three of the men that were killed that night were people I knew very well, their wives had left them home to babysit their children and went to church to attend a prayer meeting. All the men (after putting their children to sleep) went next door to play dominos and drink a few beers and ended up losing their lives. I often say to myself it could have been me. After a while, I realized that the voice heard that night was the voice of God. The scripture says, ***"my sheep listen to my voice; I know them, and they follow me." -John 10:27 (NIV)***

My sheep know my voice and another they will not follow. Always follow your instincts. You must learn to trust that still voice inside of you. God gave every one of us a spirit, and I cannot tell you how many times I have followed my instincts and got myself out of trouble or listened to a specific set of instructions from the Holy Spirit and received a financial blessing.

In 2000, I was a real estate investor and mortgage lender. I woke up one day with a desire to buy my first offshore bank. Although I had never owned a bank before or didn't even know where to start looking for a bank. My desire for a bank was great. I started to imagine myself running my new bank; I saw how owning an offshore bank would help my mortgage company grow. I thought about it long and hard and decided I wanted one; one of my plans was to attract foreign investors. One day I sat in my office and just started praying about it. I asked God if it was his will for me to own an offshore bank? If so, would He provide the money and the team that would help me to fulfill this desire? A few days later a friend of mine called me to ask for help. I asked him if he knew anything about buying an offshore bank, he told me his attorney had a client from Trinidad that owned an offshore bank and wanted me to help him find a buyer, I started to laugh. I told my friend I was interested in buying the bank, he then introduced me to his attorney who in turn introduced me to the seller. After negotiating with her I needed to come up with the first installment of a $10,000 deposit before she signed the contract. The asking price was $100,000 just for the license. I didn't know where I was going to get the money.

I assembled my team that was going to help me achieve my goal. I never thought about the cost when I was dreaming or praying for the bank. I just asked God for His will to be done. A week passed after I met the owner and found out I needed $10,000 for a down payment. I was in my office again praying and thinking about where I was going to get the money when one of my employees walked in and asked me what was on my mind. I began to tell him about this desire I had to buy an offshore bank and if I buy this bank how he was going to benefit as an employee of the company, told him owning this bank would allow us to fund loans all over the United States and we would be able to control our destiny. I told him that I need to raise some money for the down payment. He told me he didn't understand banking or half of what I said but he wished me luck and left. The next day about one o'clock in the afternoon my secretary came into my office and told me the mother of the same employee I was speaking with the day before was in the office to see me. The lady came into my office and she told me that her son had mentioned to her about my desire to buy a bank. She mentioned that she herself didn't understand anything to do with banking, but she woke up that morning with a desire to help me. The lady handed me an envelope and said this was not much but she hoped it would help. I never told her son how much I needed for the down payment but after his mother left my office I opened the envelope and inside was a check for $10,000.00 and just like that God came through for me. I was able to raise the funds I needed to buy my offshore bank.

Visualization is one of the most powerful mind exercises you can do. The bible says when we pray, "believe that you receive them, and ye shall have them."

When you are visualizing, you are emitting a powerful frequency out into the world. Athletes have been using this technique for years to improve performance.

What's the big secret to creating a Vision Board that works? Your vision board should focus on how you want to feel, not just on things you want, it's okay to include the material stuff, too. However, the more your board focuses on how you want to feel, the more it will come to life.

WHAT SHOULD YOU PUT ON YOUR VISION BOARD?

Anything that inspires, excites, and motivates you must be on your vision board. The purpose of your vision board is to bring everything on it into your life.

You should first think about your goals in the following areas: relationships, career and finances, home, travel, personal growth including spirituality, social life, education, and health.

A successful life starts with God, not with your education. Although that's important, success does not start with millions in your bank account. Although having it can create convenience in your life, true success starts with God's grace and mercy.

President Barack Obama once said *"to be successful you must first find somebody to be successful for. Raise their hopes. Think of their needs."*

Give your life purpose, you are not an accident, the color of your skin doesn't make you worthless. I cannot see my success without God. I can't see my victory without God. I can't see my future without God. There is no me without him.

CHAPTER 8

CULTIVATE PURPOSEFUL LIVING

Living a life of purpose sounds great, right? But really, what does that even mean? I strive every day to add purpose to every aspect of my life. In my opinion, giving purpose and meaning, means bringing awareness to every moment, making conscious choices, and having acceptance of the results. My actions, thoughts, and ideas are chosen on purpose (in an ideal world). This, to me, is how we live a purposeful life. Here are some simple tools that you should add into your daily routine that can help you create that purposeful life

1. Daily Meditation/Prayer. Purposeful living starts with calming the mind. Through meditation/prayer I learn to come back to myself, my thoughts begin to slow down, and I can find peace and my purpose in the present moment.

2. Be Purposeful / Set intentions. Intention-setting practices are so powerful; they create a positive ripple effect in your life. A great way to live with purpose is to set a simple goal at the beginning of each day; it actually sets the tone for your day. You choose how you want to feel and act in your day. Maybe you simply want to be happy, or be at peace, but you can feel content and at ease knowing that you can choose how to live with intent. We tend to brush through our simple daily habits without even giving them a thought. Whether it's brushing our teeth, getting dressed or even eating, we don't necessarily put thought and purpose into some of the smallest tasks. When we add importance to even the seemingly meaningless actions we then bring meaning into every action. Our purposeful life is our ordinary life!

Being purposeful, may help you live longer and stay healthier. Having a purpose can help you with decision-making and dealing with life's hardships. It would be best if you were purposeful; it would help you find what gives your life meaning. We all crave meaning and purpose in our lives, but many of us have difficulty finding it.

Be Purposeful about your life:

>If you want to save, you must be purposeful.
>If you want to come out of debt, you must be purposeful.
>If you want to fix your marriage, you must be purposeful.
>If you want to fix your family, you must be purposeful.
>If you want to be rich, you must be purposeful.
>If you want to buy a home, you must be purposeful.
>If you want to buy a new car, you must be purposeful.
>If you want to be healthy, you must be purposeful.

Being purposeful can help you with decision-making, deal with life's hardships, and provide a sense of accomplishment.

It is said, that our lives are a compilation of all the decisions we have made. If we're in a bad situation it is because of the decisions we have made. Now for some of you that does not sit well. These are often people that will not accept responsibility for where they are in life. They want to blame everyone else, they want to blame their mother, their father, their family lineage, some blame the fact they are married or not married, some blame their wife, some blame their husband.

I have a friend who believes that they are where they are now in life because they didn't have a father present in their life. The reason they think that way is because they are failing as a father with their sons. Another one of my friends tells me that he had his father in his life. Still, his father did not teach him how to be a man; he was always drunk and a bum.

These men admit that they are not doing great at being fathers, but that did not stop them from having kids with more than one woman. These men are doing to their kids the same thing their father did to them. I never met my father until I was twenty eight years old, not having him in my life when I was a young man sometimes hurt, because whenever I saw my friends hanging out with their fathers, having fun and hearing them talk about life, I use to wonder what it would be like growing up with my father. Not having a father did not stop me from not wanting to be a good father. When I got older, I decided to become the man everyone in my family said I couldn't become. I became purposeful about my life. I say all this to say that it really doesn't matter what disadvantages one may had growing up, because having a determined mindset can take you further in life than you can imagine. Once you decide who you want to become, (the type of person you want to be) and couple that with living out your purpose, you will reach heights of success for yourself you once thought unattainable.

Some of the things I implemented:

(A) I started by seeking out people that were living the life I wanted to live.

(B) I specifically searched for men that represented the type of man I wanted to become and asked them to mentor me.

To start my self-improvement journey, I had to be truthful to myself. For self-examination to be effective you first have to put your "TRUE SELF" under the microscope.

I first had to admit I was broken, imperfect, flawed, and raised in a dysfunctional home where the words "I Love You" were never spoken.

Whenever you admit that there is a problem or limitation, you will know what to start working on; whenever you decide where you want to go or what you want to be, you have to become purposeful about incorporating the things in your life that will lead you there.

Second, you must identify your heart's desire (What's your purpose). Next, you have to come up with a plan for getting there, in other words become purposeful.

If you don't have a made-up mind, you will not make it. For me, the most powerful word in the English language is "Decision," I decided what I wanted to have in my life. I decided what I would change in my life for the better. The decision I made about my life moved me to take action towards making a change.

Never look at your assignment through the lens of your wallet. Never look at your future through the lens of your family, your past experiences, or even your education. If you need to go back to school to fulfill your dreams, you must become purposeful about it. My wife and I have a non-profit organization called God's Chosen Gems. We organize two events every year. Our mission is to help people identify their purpose. When we started this organization, we didn't have any money. Every year for the first five years we would get the inspiration to do two workshops. We would pray about it and then decide on the type of events God would have us put on that year. Now when God gives an assignment that's time sensitive you have two choices. You can say "yes Lord" or "not right now Lord". When we looked at the assignment, and then looked at our wallet (there was no money in the bank) we had every reason to say "not right now Lord", BUT if you're a believer you know that God can provide all your needs. So we stepped out in faith and for five years we have put on these conference/workshops at some of the finest hotels and brought in top-level speakers. We have never done a conference that God did not pay for in full, meaning we never did a conference where we were left in the red. We took our focus off of our wallet and placed it on the assignment. God showed us ways and techniques as to how to put the conference together, how to market it, how to get sponsors, how to get people to volunteer, how to get donations and how to plan a successful conference where He got all the praise and all the glory.

> ***Where no counsel is, the people fall:***
> ***but in the multitude of counselors***
> ***there is safety -PROVERB 11: 14***

CHAPTER 9

CREATE CHANGE BY RAISING YOUR STANDARDS

When my wife and I decided that we wanted to make a difference in people's lives, we formed an organization called "God's Chosen Gems." *We made a list of all the things we would no longer accept in our own lives and within our organization. We wrote down the type of people we wanted to be, the type of business we wanted to run, the standard of excellence we wanted to set for our lives, and our business. We started shaving away everything in our lives that was not supporting the new standard we had set.* We stopped saying we couldn't, instead we said we could. There were times, we looked at our finances, and would start saying we couldn't host a conference successfully, based on the amount of money we had in our bank account, but we would catch ourselves and start to instead say "yes we can, through Christ who gives us the knowledge to do all things." If you're not in control of your mind or your belief systems, the devil will put negativity in your mind. You must believe with all your heart that he who started a good work in you is able to complete it, but you must be willing to do your part. Wishing will not bring it to pass. The trinity that's in you must be in total agreement before anything happens for you. Have you ever wondered why some believers are broke or just getting by, living from paycheck to paycheck? Doesn't God hear their prayer or see their needs? God is not moved by needs, he is moved by faith. Do you know people in your circle of life who are successful in every area of their lives, but don't know Jesus Christ as their Lord and savior? Do you ever wonder why some believers spend two, four, six or eight hours per week on their knees and are still broke? God responds to faith and faith without "works" is dead, the operative word is works. A non-believer will have confidence in his ability to complete the assignment given to him, and their God-given gift, talent, and work in faith, become successful and fulfill a purpose.

Let me explain the trinity that lives in all of us. Be purposeful, and not double-minded, the bible says a double-minded man is unstable in all his ways (James 1:8). The mind is the seat of consciousness and intellect; we then have a heart, a place of love and emotional connection, and we have an instinct (gut-feeling). We are not made to just live by our feelings but by faith. Sometimes you may not feel like working on your assignment because it looks impossible, but if your soul is right with God, your faith should tell you that you can do all things through Christ, who strengthens you. Some people, however, listen to their feelings instead of the voice of faith. Then discouragement jumps in, and stops them. Remember, you have a mind: use it. Take your doubts to the Word of God. We must learn to use our minds to watch over all matter that concerns us.

Head, Heart, and Gut, some people call it the "Three (3) Brains." If we Listen to our Gut, Follow our Heart, and Use our head, the combined wisdom will help guide you.

You probably have a sense of this already. Think about a time when you had to speak in front of a large crowd, and you felt butterflies in your stomach or knots in your belly. Or when you fell in love for the first time, and you felt it in your heart.

Listening to all three is critical in decision making. These three brains help you to make smart decisions, to avoid dangerous situations, to navigate important choices, and to spend time with people who you love. Mind.Heart.Soul.

INSPIRE YOURSELF

Your life is yours to design. The giant within you lies inside a mustard seed. Jesus said: ***"The kingdom of heaven is like to a grain of mustard seed, which a man took, and sowed in his field: Which indeed is the least of all seeds: but when it is grown, it is the greatest among herbs, and become a tree, so that the birds of the air come and lodged in the branches thereof." Matthew 13: 31 -33.***

Your purpose should fulfill a need in the Kingdom. Be careful of what you allow to enter your eye gate, your ear gate, and what comes out of your mouth gate. Be cautious of the words you speak into the garden of your mind and your heart. Words are like seeds if you allow the wrong type of seed to get into your garden and don't remove them immediately by casting them down and rebuking the source of negative ones. They will grow or you will start to believe what the naysayers are saying about you. They already think you can't make it, they already think you're no good, they already think you're worthless, they already think you won't come out to anything. You MUST CAST THOSE THOUGHTS DOWN. Motivate yourself, learn to be a self-motivator.

Value your time—always remember that you only have a limited period of time on this earth. Success won't just happen; you have to work for it, set a standard of excellence in everything you do. Anyone can achieve success if they go after their dreams purposefully.

Finally, brethren, whatsoever things are true, whatsoever things are honest, whatsoever things are just, whatsoever things are pure, whatsoever things are lovely, whatsoever things are of good report; if there be any virtue, and if there be any praise, think on these things (Philippians 4:8).

Seeds grow to become trees. Seeds grow after their kind, every thought felt as true or allow to be accepted as true by your conscious mind takes root in your subconscious and blossoms sooner or later. It will bear fruit after its kind. Good thoughts brings forth good fruit, whatsoever things are lovely, whatsoever things are of good report, whatsoever is positive, whatsoever is uplifting whatsoever excites you whatsoever motivates you, think on these things.

Think about the consequences of your action; if you don't pursue your dream or purpose, where will you be in ten years. Imagine what your life will look like twenty years into the future, if continued on the road you're on right now. Would you get to where you wanted to be?

I remember a time when my life was not going in the direction I wanted it to go. I was also working in a job I didn't like, I had a boss I didn't get along with. I started to wonder if this was what my life was going to look like in twenty years. One dead end job to another without any purpose. For a short time I accepted that position because I told myself I needed the money, I had bills to pay. I needed to keep a roof over my head and food on my table, and I also needed to have my party money. This went on for about five years, until one day for no reason I got fired from my job. The boss I didn't like, didn't like me either. She had me escorted off the property by security. That experience humiliated me so much I decided right there and then I was going to change my life. That experience motivated me to action.

What is your excuse for not taking action right now? What will it take to move towards your goal? You don't have to quit your job right away.

Start working on your dream part time. We all need a job so we can feed our family. Start going after your dream in your spare time or whenever you can but start to take action. How fast or slow you get to start living your dream depends on how much time you put into it.

If the job you're presently doing is where your purpose is being fulfilled, start thinking of creative ways to make your job better, think of creative ways you can add more value to the company from the position you're in. Companies are looking for employees that show initiative. People don't lack time to work on their dreams, they lack motivation.

> ***Give her the product of her hands, and let her***
> ***works praise her in the gates.***
> ***Proverbs 31:31***

Make your life count before you die. Decide now what you want, plan your goal, give birth to your purpose, decide right now what you want your life to be about. Decide on your destination. Where you see yourself in five years, ten years or twenty years.

Remember the sermon on the mount, "Ask and it will be given to you; seek and you will find; knock and the door will be opened to you. For everyone who asks receives; he who seeks finds; and to him who knocks, the door will be opened." Step out on faith. Change your mind, change your life. We become what we think about. Your mind is your greatest on tap resource. The greatest achievement was at first a dream. Always remember the oak tree sleeps in the acorn. Your vision is the promise of what you shall one day be, as you believe so shall it be done unto you.

Oftentimes, people allow the opinions of others to hold them down or discourage them and cause them to lose confidence. They may give up on their dreams or put them on the shelf and never look at them again, but, we have to realize that there will always be critics and naysayers in life. One of the most important things you can learn is that other people don't have to believe in you for your dreams to come true.

People don't set the limits for your life – YOU DO! It's not what others say about you that affects your life, but what you say and believe about yourself. When God puts a promise in your heart, it's not up to other people to bring it to pass, it's up to you!

The Apostle Paul is saying, "It doesn't matter if other people don't believe. Their unbelief is not going to keep me from believing in my dreams." You don't need other people to validate you. You only have to know God for yourself and allow Him to order your steps.

> *"If you want to change your life, you have to raise your standards."—Tony Robbins*

I remember when I first heard the phrase "Changed Mind, Changed Life" I learned that the quality of my life is a reflection of the standards I set for myself.

If you win a million dollars in the lottery and still have a poverty mindset, you will be broke in no time. Being poor is not about making less money. Being poor is a mentality. It's a choice to live a low standard of life. When I say low standard, I don't mean the luxuries and pleasures that rich people can afford.

You can raise your standards regardless of how much money you make. It's not about money, it's about mindset. Different people have different values. We can have high standards in some areas of our lives while we may avoid other areas.

The five major areas of life where you can raise your standards is:

- **Health:** If you want to build up your health, start to exercise; go for a walk.
- **Relationships:** Set a standard about the type of people you want in your life.
- **Mindset:** (The way you look at life) a changed mind produces a changed life.
- **Wealth:** If you want to raise your wealth standards, learn to manage your finances.
- **Self-discipline:** Develop habits that will move you toward your purpose.

After my first marriage ended, I met with a good friend of mine, Dr. Portman, a Psychologist. He asked me about my wife and I told him we got a divorce. I started by telling him what went wrong in our marriage. He asked me what I was looking for in a woman? I began to describe her physical attributes as well as her mental capabilities, after he listened to me rambling on about this perfect woman he asked me a question that forever changed the way I look at my relationship with women, with people and with life. The question was, "Why would the perfect woman I just described want to marry me?" This question sent me on a journey of self-examination and self-discovery. I started realizing that if I wanted good things in my life or wanted my life to change, I would have first to become the very thing that would attract that which I wanted. In other words if I wanted a good wife or what some would call my soul-mate I would have to first live by the standards that a woman of that quality would want to marry. I started living by this idea eighteen years ago. I met my current wife two years after that and now we have been married for sixteen years with three kids. Keep in mind I didn't say perfect life, but I eventually found someone who will walk through life with me, for good or bad, in sickness or health, until death we will part, and til this day, I live by the standards I set for myself.

CHAPTER 10

FIGHTING THE GOOD FIGHT OF FAITH

He killed lions and bears, and he also killed animals that were much bigger and stronger than himself. Because of the battles he had been through, David learned to trust God. David developed Great Faith in God because of the numerous challenges he had to endure. In God, there was no reason for him to be afraid of Goliath. Likewise, with God on our side, we can be fearless—afraid of "no one" or "no thing."

Being human means we each struggle with some degree of fear. However when we are going through trials, and the temptation to fear becomes great, we must keep in mind that God has not deserted us. Everyone has been given a measure of faith to live this Christian life. Trials become the place where we exercise this gift. When we choose to follow Christ our entire life becomes a journey of faith. Ephesians 2:8-9 explains that faith is a free gift ***"For by grace are we*** *saved through faith, and that not of yourselves, it is the gift of God: not a result of works, so that no one may boast."*

The word Faith and Fight are words that go hand in hand. The bible says we must fight the good fight of faith. To fight the good fight of faith means that we abide in the Word by faith, regardless of what we feel or what we think we understand. Jesus said, *"If you abide in my word, you are my disciples indeed." -John 8:31*

I often wonder the purpose conflict, trials, or hard times can have in my life? In the end, after I have overcome them, I can often see how God used them to build my spiritual muscles (my faith muscle).

David was a shepherd boy protecting his father's flock of sheep; he had to fight off lions and bears to keep his flock safe. David knew without a doubt that God was with him! The Lord was building courage and faith in him through the trials he had to face. In like manner, we must also respond to the challenges in our lives out of faith, not fear!

I now rest assured knowing that the same God who was with me in the past, when I faced my greatest battles is with me again. Like David I declare, *"The Lord who saved me from the claws of the lion and the bear will save me from this Philistine!" -1 Samuel 17:37*

> *"Great faith is the product of great fights. Great testimonies are the outcome of great tests. Great triumphs can only come out of great trials."*
> Smith Wigglesworth

Life is unpredictable. There is no straight path to success on your desired destination. You have to go through all the different phases in life's journey before you reach your goal. The twist and turns in life make up the experiences that life gives. Our lives (meaning these experiences) are where we learn our most valuable lessons.

The great fight in life is built in the faith. Therefore, we have to overcome each hurdle we encounter with confidence. To keep our faith strong, we need to understand that it's about never giving up! Not everything we touch will turn to gold or turn out as planned and because we pray doesn't mean we will get an immediate answer. But if we keep believing in the promises of God and never give up, then in His time, we will get to where He wants us to be.

All of us, believers and non-believers alike, are built to experience victory in our lives. From time-to-time, we need to review the owner's manual, "the Bible," to remember how to keep our faith strong during tough times.

Practicing faith takes action. Faith requires us to think, feel, and believe. Some of us expect our faith to arrive without any deliberate intent on our part, and then we run the risk of missing the chance to live the life we desire. Pray about what actions you should take to get the desired results you want, rather than fall to external pressures.

Your action and involvement, create tangible results that allow you to see that your faith is alive and strong. Like everything else we do, we get better at something the more we do it. Practicing and using our faith is no different.

HOW DO WE FIGHT THE GOOD FIGHT OF FAITH?

The Bible says we must fight the good fight of faith. Living in this world isn't easy and when we watch the news, we can see that we are in a fight; it's a war! It is a long, hard battle for our very soul, and this battle requires endurance.

The Bible says, **Fight the good fight of the faith. Take hold of the eternal life to which you were called and about which you made the good confession in the presence of many witnesses. -1 Timothy 6:12**

One reason following Jesus is described as a fight, is because we have a real enemy:

We must be sober-minded and watchful. Your adversary, the devil, prowls around like a roaring lion, seeking someone to devour. 1 Peter 5:8

FIGHT THROUGH TRIALS

We cannot always control everything that happens to us in this life, but we can control how we respond. Many struggles come as problems and pressures that sometimes cause pain. Others come as temptations, trials, and tribulations.

In this world of opposition in all things, life is not fair. The real question we need to ask ourselves is, "When sorrow, misfortune, or tragedy strikes, how will we respond?"

Faith should be a part of our resume. People are always asking to review their resume or write their resume. If I look at your resume as a believer, will we see a life of FAITH?

On the journey of your life, did you develop faith? Have you been through anything that you know if it were not for your faith in God, you would not have made it through? You would not of been healed? Your marriage would be in shambles? Your finances would be all messed up?

It is my belief that the journey of life was not made to be easy, for if it were, we would not learn to have faith.

A GREAT FIGHT IS A PRODUCT OF GREAT FAITH.

We will have tribulation and trouble in our lives. Believers suffer in all kinds of ways. Believers are persecuted in many ways. We will be betrayed by both unbelievers and believers, family, and even some friends.

We will love and receive hatred in return. We will be accused of things unjustly. We will be misunderstood. We will get sick. We will be rejected, even at times by those we love.

And in these times of suffering, we have to fight. We have to fight, primarily to hold fast to our Lord in faith. We have to fight to believe His word. We have to fight not to accept the lies of the enemy.

FIGHT FOR JOY AND PEACE

We have to fight to have joy and peace. We have to fight to trust the Lord. We have to fight to keep going. We have to fight to love our enemies , to do good to those who abuse us and to bless those who curse us. We have to fight not to grow cold in our love for Jesus.

HOW DO WE FIGHT THE GOOD FIGHT OF FAITH?

Finally, be strong in the Lord and in the strength of his might. Put on the whole armor of God, that you may be able to stand against the schemes of the devil."For we do not wrestle against flesh and blood, but against the rulers, against the authorities, against the cosmic powers over this present darkness, against the spiritual forces of evil in the heavenly places. Therefore take up the whole armor of God, that you may be able to withstand in the evil day, and having done all, to stand firm. Stand therefore, having fastened on the belt of truth, and having put on the breastplate of righteousness, and, as shoes for your feet, having put on the readiness given by the gospel of peace. In all circumstances take up the shield of faith, with which you can extinguish all the flaming darts of the evil one; and take the helmet of salvation, and the sword of the Spirit, which is the word of God, praying at all times in the Spirit, with all prayer and supplication.

To that end, keep alert with all perseverance, making supplication for all the saints, and also for me, that words may be given to me in opening my mouth boldly to proclaim the mystery of the gospel, for which I am an ambassador in chains, that I may declare it boldly, as I ought to speak."
-Ephesians 6:10

WE MUST BE STRONG IN THE LORD.

We can't fight the good fight on our own. We just aren't strong enough. We need the Lord's strength. We need his might, calling out to him, asking him to help us, asking him for his strength.

Humble yourselves, therefore, under the mighty hand of God so that at the proper time he may exalt you, casting all your anxieties on him, because he cares for you.
-1 Peter 5:6-7

It's humbling to admit that we are weak, that we need help. But, that's exactly what God tells us to do. He says, don't try to fight this fight on your own; cast your cares and anxieties on the Lord. Humble yourself. Cry out to God!

In Ephesians 6 Paul tells us that to be able to fight the good fight of faith and stand against our enemies, we must put on God's armor, including the "belt of truth," "the shield of faith" and "the sword of the Spirit, which is the word of God." Why? Because Satan's primary weapon is his lies. Just as he lied to Eve: "Did God really say?...You will not die."

WE MUST BELIEVE IN THE PROMISES OF GOD

When we are going through a hard time Satan will whisper, "No one cares about you. No one is going to come to your rescue. God isn't with you in this one. This is too big for God."

In these times of temptation, we doubt God's word. We must become purposeful in fighting the good fight of faith. How did Jesus fight the enemy? We should do what Jesus did when the devil tempted him. Jesus' response was the written Word. He quoted the Holy Scripture. This is how we should fight the good fight of faith. By reminding ourselves of God's promises and believing them. By standing in the faith that what God has promised us in His word will come to pass in our lives.

When we are tempted to fear for our children or be discouraged about their lack of faith, we must cling to God's many promises to work in our children's lives.

> ***All your children shall be taught***
> ***by the LORD, and great shall be***
> ***the peace of your children.***
> ***-Isaiah 54:13***

God's word is the truth, "the belt of truth" no matter what our circumstances look like. Our feelings aren't the truth. The lies of the enemy are his "fiery darts" which we extinguish by lifting up, "the shield of faith" faith in God's word, and brandishing "the sword of the Spirit, which is the word of God."

WE MUST PRAY AT ALL TIMES

We need to pray for strength. We need to pray for joy. Pray for wisdom and guidance. Pray for God to deliver us from temptation and evil. Pray that God will help us love those who hurt us.

Prayer is a form of "sowing" seeds. And like seeds, sometimes it takes a while before we see the harvest. But, we must keep sowing in faith, for God promises us: ***Those who sow in tears shall reap with shouts of joy! He who goes out weeping, bearing the seed for sowing, shall come home with shouts of joy, bringing his sheaves with him. -Psalm 126:5-6***

Keep praying those prayers. Because someday, and we don't know when, but someday we will "come home with shouts of joy" bringing a harvest of "sheaves" of answered prayers with us.

PRAY FOR OTHERS AND HAVE THEM PRAY FOR YOU

To that end, keep alert with all perseverance, making supplication for all the saints, and also for me, that words may be given to me in opening my mouth boldly to proclaim the mystery of the gospel... (Ephesians 6:18-19)

We're not in this fight by ourselves. We need our brothers and sisters to pray for us, and we need to pray for them. The Apostle Paul humbly asked for his brothers and sisters to pray for him. He asked that they pray for him to be bold to proclaim the gospel.

We fight the good fight of faith every day. We fight by

dying to ourselves and obeying Jesus. We fight the good fight by serving, loving, and encouraging others. By sharing the gospel with others. By giving to the poor and in many other ways.

Fighting isn't easy. War is hard. Following Jesus is work. But what joy our fight will yield when we hear Jesus say, "Well done, good and faithful servant. So don't give up! Remember, a great fight is the product of great faith!

CHAPTER 11

PAY ATTENTION!

Please pay attention to your words; they can change your life. The words we choose to speak to ourselves or others have the power to positively or negatively impact others and ourselves. When we lose focus, and our attention gets drawn away from what we know, the direction changes. Our life veers off course. Our words or language often follow suit. We start speaking negatively.

Write down or memorize a set of promises God made to you in his word (The Bible) and stand on it; use it to help you stay the course. The word of God will lift your spirit, empower you, ignite passion, present purpose, and enlighten the way for those around you.

When paying attention, you need to be able to survey your life and see what God has called you to do and how to get you where you want to be. Sometimes we miss God, because we are simply not paying attention. If God is the head of your life, then he should be leading your life, the word says He will make you lay down in green pastures and lead you beside still waters. He will restore your soul. He also said that you should prosper as your soul prospers. So if God is leading you, you will see prosperity in your life.

We must not rely on instinct or intuition, but rely only on the Holy Spirit. He will lead you into all truths.

Paying attention is how I survived my childhood and my teenage years. I was raised by multiple family members and at times even by strangers. Every time I moved to a new home I had to learn how to navigate my new surroundings. I had to learn about the likes and dislikes of the new people I was living with; each household did things differently. Some people were physically abusive while some were verbally abusive, in some homes the living conditions were somewhat comfortable while others were rough and extremely uncomfortable. If I paid attention, I would always find a way to make my living conditions tolerable.

The same habit works great in my Christian life. If I pay attention to God and listen to his word, I always get good results. Jesus said in the Bible "I am the vine you (and I) are the branches. If we abide in him and he abides in us we will produce fruit but without Him (Jesus Christ) we can do nothing.

God wants to have a relationship with us. He wants to be the number one person we go to when we run into problems, when we are afraid or need someone to talk to. God wants dialogue. More times than not, we choose to turn to family or our friends instead. We sometimes lean on our own understanding and forget that God is there for us. God is always trying to get our attention.

Another thing we must do is pay attention to the words we allow to proceed from our mouths. We must speak positive words that inspire us. We should also read stories that encourage us, motivate us, and uplift us. We need to speak words that bring peace to our heart.

If two people make peace together in a single house, they will say to this mountain move and go elsewhere and it will. Our words have power. Do you agree with the words you say about yourself? Are those words uplifting? Are those words encouraging? Do your words bring healing to your body? If not, you should change the words you're speaking by paying attention to the words coming out of your mouth. Out of the abundance of the heart, the mouth speaks. If you're hurting, then it's fair to say you will speak words that hurt. You will speak negative words about your life. I am sure you know the phrase "Hurt people, hurt people."

FOOD FOR THOUGHT

Blessed the lion that the human may devour so the lion becomes human and cursed is the human that the lion devours so the lion becomes human (spiritual metaphor) . It's all about our true nature. If we take on the true nature of a lion we will become furious and stronger. Lion is the symbol of courage, personal strength, and power. Each individual should endeavor to adopt the spiritual traits that will enable them to live the life they so desire. In this proverb, man is symbolized as a predator, animal, inventor of the negativity, and separated from his natural condition by instruments of his own making.

There is another old proverb that says *"An army of sheep led by a lion can defeat an army of lions led by a sheep."*

THE KINGDOM OF GOD IS INSIDE OF YOU

When we make the two, one, when thought and emotion become one, it removes doubt. If the two make peace together in this one house (we are the house we are the temple) if thought and emotion become one and make peace, you will say to the mountain move away and it will.

The Bible says ask, and you will receive. How does this work?

(Answer) Without doubt. How do you remove doubt? By believing the word of God, by your prayers, and by your faith. Believing the word of God. By feeling it in your heart with no doubt in your mind (mind and heart coming together as one) that's what you're saying is true even if there is no immediate evidence (faith) that you already have it. Take the position of it in your Spirit, in your heart. Ask that you may receive so your joy may be full. So you should have joy if you believe in your heart that God has already given you what you ask for. Then your action should start clearing the way for the manifestation of what you asked for because your prayers have already been answered (be surrounded by your answer in your thoughts and in your spirit) ask without judging yourself whether you deserve it or not.

PAY ATTENTION

Make your future dream a present reality " by "believing the feeling (the belief) of your prayer fulfilled. When you pray believe it has been done, and it shall be done, pay attention!

Paying attention simply means being attentive. As simple as this may sound, paying attention is what helped me grow up. Our power of observation is more powerful than we think and all we have to do in order to grow is pay attention to our surroundings or to how we speak or to who or what we listen to, or to what type of information we are feeding ourselves.

Whether good or bad, the experiences we go through in life should be embraced.

THREE WAYS GOD TRIES TO GET OUR ATTENTION.

Through His Word: The Word Convicts You. I am so thankful I have the Word of God, that reveals the will of God. I'm also grateful for the Holy Spirit that speaks to me and illuminates the Holy Scriptures. As a believer, we know the word of God is living and active, sharper than any two-edged sword, piercing to the division of soul and spirit, and of joints and of marrow, and discerns the thoughts and intentions of the heart" (Hebrews 4:12). If you read a bible verse that convicts you, God may be trying to tell you something and is using His written word to do it. Whenever God convicts us he is trying to get our attention.

Through the Fire: Some of us go through a trial. Trials can strengthen our faith in God, and deepen our dependence on Him, both of which are great. God allows trials "so that they test the genuineness of our faith."

It's not meant to harm you, but to help you and strengthen your trust in Him because when you come out of the fiery furnace, you'll see how God is purifying and growing you.

The voice of others: God sometimes uses the voice of other believers to speak to us. That's what the primary role of the prophet was in the Old Testament. They spoke for God and spoke the Words of God. It was, "Thus says the Lord," and not "Thus says Pastor so and so." So your friends may not be speaking the Word of God or a word from God, but they might be speaking the wisdom of God as revealed in Scripture. God may sometimes use a friend to speak some sense into us. It is absolutely true that ***"Faithful are the wounds of a friend; profuse are the kisses of an enemy" -Prov 27:6***. If we ignore godly advice from those brothers and sisters around us, we do so to our own peril. Before we shrug off a fellow believer's comment, think about it, they might be right. If they are, confess it to God and admit it to your friend, and say, "Thank you for valuing me enough to tell me the truth." God's Word comforts the afflicted and afflicts the comfortable.

Every day, choose to speak words that make others feel valuable. Create conversations that are positive and make the people you interact with everyday feel as if they matter. Paying Attention will drastically improve your life.

CHAPTER 12

CHOOSING THE TRUTH

Sadly, some of us have lost our moral compass. As Christians, our moral compass "is the only thing that tells which direction we should go when making decisions involving right and wrong. This moral compass ought to be built upon our Christian beliefs. As believers, we should strive to see things from Jesus' perspective. This requires that we orient ourselves with the word of God, continually. We have to ask ourselves, am I following Jesus? I am doing what He expects of me? Am I in the place where He leads me?

It seems evangelicals today have chosen Barabbas and thrown out the truth and the light. Some believers are fighting from their faith on every front. It seems the world has been turned upside down, and we have become a nation of people that believe we should have all our opinions heard without any restraint, (no matter how crazy they may be). Social media has given us the medium to display our ideas; the good and bad. As believers in Jesus Christ, we have been asked to question our faith, values, and belief systems as far as policies are concerned. Requesting us to choose, Barabbas or Jesus, and unfortunately many good-hearted believers have been tricked by their leaders, and mainstream media, and have unknowingly chosen Barabbas. They tell us to put our Bibles down, get politically correct, and fight for our country; the same government that removed God from our schools is the same country that wants to govern the way we preach the Word and the way we live.

Barabbas means "Son of the father," Let us examine who the Bible says he was. For those of you who never heard of Barabbas he was. The Bible says Barabbas was a "popular prisoner"; everyone knew who he was. Other writers of the gospel refer to Barabbas as one involved in public disruption aka "riots," probably, "one of the numerous insurrections against the Roman power" He was said to have committed murder and was put in prison by the Romans, Barabbas is called a "notorious prisoner."

We will look at three characteristics that define the Barabbas syndrome and identify how it has taken over America.

1. Popular prisoner
2. Public disruption "riots."
3. Barabbas was not a common criminal.

Barabbas was what I call an insurrectionist - Dictionary definition and meaning for word insurrectionist: (Noun) *A person who takes part in an armed rebellion against the constituted authority (especially hoping to improve conditions).*

When we hear religious leaders claiming God told them this person or that one is supposed to be our next leader, we must examine the prophecy. Jesus warned, **"Many will say to me on that day, 'Lord, Lord, did we not prophesy in your name and in your name drive out demons and in your name perform many miracles?' Then I will tell them plainly, 'I never knew you. Away from me, you evildoers!'" Matthew 7:22-23**

Barabbas's name means the son of God, his full name was Yeshua Barabbas. Yeshua means Jesus, son of God, and Yeshua also means Joshua. Having a name like Yeshua Barabbas did not make him the coming messiah. Jesus fulfills every prophecy that was spoken about him, and it is His moral character that we strive to live up to.

We, as a people, have been looking for a change for some time. We are still looking in the wrong places because we believe if we pick the right politician (Right Leader), we will be a great nation, and we are making the same mistake the Israelites made in the old testament. When they chose Saul they said they wanted to be like other nations, therefore they wanted a king.

SAMUEL'S WARNING AGAINST KINGS

So Samuel told all the words of the Lord to the people who were asking for a king from him. He said, "These will be the ways of the king who will reign over you: he will take your sons and appoint them to his chariots and to be his horsemen and to run before his chariots. And he will appoint for himself commanders of thousands and commanders of fifties, and some to plow his ground and to reap his harvest, and to make his implements of war and the equipment of his chariots. He will take your daughters to be perfumers and cooks and bakers. He will take the best of your fields and vineyards and olive orchards and give them to his servants. He will take the tenth of your grain and your vineyards and give it to his officers and his servants. He will take your male servants and female servants and the best of your young men and your donkeys and put them to his work. He will take the tenth of your flocks, and you shall be his slaves. And in that day you will cry out because of your king, whom you have chosen for yourselves, but the Lord will not answer you in that day." -1 Samuel 8:10-18

THE LORD GRANTS ISRAEL'S REQUEST

But the people refused to obey the voice of Samuel. And they said, "No! But there shall be a king over us, that we also may be like all the nations, and that our king may judge us and go out before us and fight our battles." And when Samuel had heard all the words of the people, he repeated them in the ears of the Lord. And the Lord said to Samuel, "Obey their voice and make them a king." Samuel then said to the men of Israel, "Go every man to his city." 1 Samuel 8:19-22 (KJV)

Now Jesus stood before the governor; and the governor asked him, Are you the King of the Jews? Jesus said you say so. But when he was accused by the chief priests and elders, he did not answer. Then Pilate said to him, do you not hear how many accusations they make against you? But he gave him no answer, not even to a single charge, so that the governor was greatly amazed. Now at the festival the governor was accustomed to release a prisoner for the crowd, anyone whom they wanted. At that time they had a notorious prisoner, called Jesus Barabbas. So after they had gathered,

Pilate said to them, whom do you want me to release for you? Barabbas or Jesus who is called the Messiah? for he realized that it was out of jealousy that they had handed him over. While he was sitting on the judgment seat, his wife sent word to him, Have nothing to do with that innocent man, for today I have suffered a great deal because of a dream about him. Now the chief priests and the elders persuaded the crowds to ask for Barabbas and to have Jesus killed. The governor again said to them, which of the two do you want me to release for you? They said, Barabbas. Pilate said to them, and then what should I do with Jesus who is called the Messiah? All of them said, Let him be crucified! Then he asked, why, what evil has he done? But they shouted all the more, Let him be crucified! So when Pilate saw that he could do nothing, but rather that a riot was beginning, he took some water and washed his hands before the crowd, saying, I am innocent of this man's blood; see to it yourselves. Then the people as a whole answered, His blood will be on us and on our children! So he released Barabbas for them; and after flogging Jesus, he handed him over to be crucified. -Matthew 27:11-26

HIS BLOOD WILL BE UPON US.

As a country, America has made some bad choices for the wrong reasons. Now the question we are asking ourselves is what is the cost we pay to get the judges we want and to have the American embassy moved to Jerusalem? We have sold our souls for political positioning. Our Christian morals or the character of Jesus Christ that we are supposed to live by doesn't seem to be as important to some evangelicals. How can we say we are followers of Christ and support the immoral conduct of our present leaders?

As a Christian, I am standing for holiness. I am standing

for righteousness. Those two character traits are still important to my Christian faith.

Life can be hard sometimes, routine shifting to something new, conflict with others, or moments in life turning out to be less than ideal. We all confront seasons in life that cause us to come face to face with disappointments. It's in these moments when our heads are hung low, and it takes all the winds out of our sails. We must learn to encourage ourselves, despair likes to sing its sad song. "It will tell you that you will never be good enough, or you don't have what it takes to win the battle. You always tell yourself you are good enough, and you win; there's no going back. It's no time to give up." The bad news is that the battle has just begun. There is an enemy out there that will feed us lies and try to take away our hope, who tells us we are unworthy and incapable. When those lies are believed, the enemy knows that there is no forward progression and we lose hope, but there is good news. The answer is "be strong," Believe in yourself, choose the right words to empower yourself.

Winston Churchill once said, *"Short words are best, and old words, when short, are best of all.*

CHAPTER 13

MARRIAGE: LIVING HAPPILY EVER AFTER

Every person who is married can testify that marriage is a ministry. The Bible says, He who finds a wife finds a good thing and obtains the favor of GOD. If you want to have a happy and fulfilled marriage, spend as much time serving each other. Marriages depend on communication, sacrifice, and honesty. The word teaches husbands to love their wives the way Christ loves the church. It never says the wife should love her husband. As a husband, I strive to meet my spouse's needs before meeting the needs of others. I encourage every couple to have a marriage plan; if you're going to have a plan for your business, you should have one for your marriage, for your ministry and your life.

I never predicted that the most challenging part of parenting is that our children come to fully understand that they are the third person in our marriage. This arrangement began roughly as soon as they learned to talk.

People get so caught up in the excitement of their wedding planning that it can be hard to imagine that you and your spouse might not live happily ever after. But sharing your life with another person can be a challenge, especially if you don't have a lot of experience with marriage. Marriages take work, commitment, and love, but they also need mutual respect to be truly happy and prosperous.

A marriage based on love and respect doesn't just happen. Both spouses have to do their part. There are some important things we must work on every day to make marriage successful: We must understand that's it's ok to disagree.

> *Learn to forgive each other.*
> *Continually work on building trust.*
> *Make quality time for each other.*
> *Communicate clearly and often.*
> *Show you appreciate each other often.*

Couples talk about how romantic their relationship was before getting married and how hard it has become now that they are married. Some of the reasons are that kids are now in the mix, and everything becomes a little more stressful, and there is less time for romance. This experience is so common that it's practically universal, yet it's not commonly discussed among couples. Many couples expect that adding children to the mix will bring them closer together, and that may happen in some ways, but often not in the ways that a couple might expect.

While we don't want this to be true, many people find that children create significant stress in a relationship, particularly when they are young. Still, they also bring a tremendous amount of joy and unconditional love.

My wife and I have been married for 16 years and one thing I notice is the different seasons we go through in our lives; there are times we are going through the same season as a couple and another time we are going through a season as individuals.

I define good seasons as periods in life when things are going well for the most part. Everything seems OK; business is good, clients are coming in, marriage is good, we are loving each other, we haven't had a disagreement in weeks, kids are doing great, and things are harmonious. We are moving forward as a couple and as a family. Without warning the season changes, business begins struggling, money starts looking funny, it's not flowing in the abundance it was, you might have money stashed away for a rainy day, but the atmosphere is affected by the lack of money coming into the home. There are other times when things are going great with me and the season in my wife's life changes and everything on my wife's job is going crazy. She is frustrated and aggravated with the job and everything she is feeling finds its way into our home. She might be short with me and the kids or easily get upset because of little things that usually wouldn't bother her.

I have learned that no matter what season we are going through, the family must move forward. There are things my wife and I are working towards as a family, and no matter the season, we never take our eyes off the goal as a family. If I am going through a rough patch, my wife's strength, the encouragement of my wife, the prayers of my wife, and my wife's love, all keep me moving forward, and the same goes for me as her husband. If the captain of an army is wounded on the battlefield does he stop being the captain? NO, as long as he is capable he is still sending instruction out to the battlefield where the soldiers are fighting, because his mission whether he is sick or wounded, is to win the battle. As a husband it does not matter who is in front as long as I know my position and operate from that position. I recall a time when business was really bad, my company was not doing well, and the only real income coming into our home was my wife's. I didn't lose my position as the head of my family because my wife was bringing home the bacon, NO, I continued to pray for her every day. I prayed for her job that God would bless the owners of the company. I prayed for blessings upon her boss, blessings over her co-workers and prayed that God would continue to show her uncommon favor on that job. I prayed for cooperation and peace in her work environment. As a husband and partner to my wife, no matter what condition I find myself in, the duties of my position have not changed, my duty is not defined by the amount of money I bring home, or whatever season we are going through, husband means the head of household. I remember the story of Jesus. The scripture said His mother, Mary, was pledged to be married to Joseph, but before they came together, she was found to be with child through the Holy Spirit. Because Joseph, her husband, was a righteous man he did not want to expose her to public disgrace. This meant he knew his position and the duties of that position and his first thought was to protect her. He thought that by divorcing her quietly she would not be subjected to disgrace and shame, but an angel of the Lord revealed to him the purpose of their union and how important it was for him to honor his commitment to Mary, because God's purpose was going to be fulfilled through their marriage. As a couple, we have to always remember that God brings us together for a purpose, and no matter what the season is, HIS purpose must be fulfilled in our lives. So, we must not only know our positions, but how to operate from them with love.

When two individuals are married they become one flesh. They enter into marriage with their individual dreams and desires. It becomes important that they find a way to merge those dreams and desires into one, so no one feels they are giving up on their dreams for the other person as this may ultimately lead to feelings of being unfulfilled in the union. When I met my wife she was living out one of her dreams, she had an organization called God's Chosen Gems, their purpose was to help women find their purpose. I also had an organization called the United Crusader Ministry. Our objective was to help the church fulfill its purpose in the community by organizing community outreach programs and inviting all the churches to work together to meet the needs of the people. One day after we were married I was in my prayer room and I heard the Holy Spirit say that a marriage will never move forward with two visions, to find a way to merge both our visions into one. I instinctively desired to create a motto that my marriage and our family would live by. I told my wife that we needed to have a meeting about our future in two weeks; I scheduled an appointment with my wife for two weeks in advance and began to pray. I needed guidance as to how to structure our life. The first scripture that came to mind was **"Unless the Lord builds the house, they labor in vain who build it" -Psalm 127:1**

The first thing the Holy Spirit did was to show me how to merge the two organizations into one, my first instincts were to put everything under my organization because mine was established over a longer period of time, but after much prayer, the Lord instructed me to build everything under my wife's company.

Now as a man my ego stepped in, and said "No" she should follow me because I am the head of my family, but the

Lord said you could do it my way or your way, so I choose His way and I never regretted it. God has blessed our ministry over and beyond what we expected. The purpose is not realized when husbands and wives are traveling separate paths "unequally yoked" as they start pulling in different directions.

It's funny that we plan for our wedding but don't plan for our marriage; we even have rules on having a happy marriage, but not a plan for our married life together. The only goal some people have is how many kids they want to have.

Here are some topics each person should have in their marriage plan :

- Family meetings. Set aside time to talk about things that are important to the family
- Family Motto. What's the motto for your family? The purpose of a motto is to remind each person of the foundational beliefs that create the foundation they live by as a family.
- Date night
- Bible study/family devotions
- Daily Prayer. A couple that prays together stays together.
- Parenting Plan. How you will raise your children
- Financial Plan. How you will budget and invest
- Bank accounts. How they will be managed.
- AND... Never ever stop opening the car door for your wife after your married

> *Do not be yoked together with unbelievers.*
> *For what do righteousness and wickedness have in*
> *common? Or what fellowship can light have with*
> *darkness? -2 Corinthians 6:14 (NIV)*

The scripture says do not be yoked together with unbelievers; you can be unequally yoked in your ideas as a couple, and in your vision for your family, if you don't believe in your spouse's vision you are unequally yoked. Husbands and wives must write down each other's dreams and desires. For you to succeed as a couple, you must agree to merge your goals in life and create one vision.

> *Can two walk together,*
> *except they be agreed?*
> *Amos 3:3 (KJV)*

Marriage is more than just a physical union; it is also a spiritual and emotional union. If you are married, you may have discovered why marriage is so important and may have experienced some of the good that comes from being married. Or, maybe marriage was hard for some of you, and you're no longer married. However, there is hope. But that hope starts with realizing that marriage can be more amazing than you have experienced or even thought.

I've been married many years and have experienced both the amazing as well as the extremely challenging. However, I have come to realize we are way more effective in working as a team versus working as individuals. Through challenges, we have both matured. As a side bonus, we have wonderful kids that came from our union, but I've also discovered something even more significant. I believe God has created marriage to reveal more about Himself and how awesome He is.

The fact that marriage is an act of service makes it a ministry. First, you serve God in your marriage by loving each other and loving Him. Your service is the exercising of vows you promised to keep in His presence to your spouse. Every time you pray for your spouse and with your spouse you are engaged in ministry.

CHAPTER 14

MINISTRY: THE GREAT COMMISSION

Some of us believe that the only time we can serve in ministry is when we hold a church position, like a Deacon, Bishop, Evangelist, Minister, Prophetess, or Pastor. Some of us believe that only pastors serve because they are the ones they see on television or on the internet, they are the ones being asked to travel the world to preach the gospel, they are the ones on the pulpit every Sunday morning bringing the word. We forget the great commission, "Go into the entire world and preach the gospel to all creation." Christ gave every believer this command, that's the job each and every one of us has.

Your life is your ministry; your life is the testimony, your history, your story. When I look back at where I came from and where I am today, I know without a shadow of a doubt it was all God's goodness. I know each one of us has a story, a story of victory, a story of survival, a story of overcoming.

Check your life, God MUST have brought you through something, God must have delivered you from something. So we cannot say we don't have a ministry! Share your story.

WHAT HAS GOD DONE FOR YOU? I remember being in a club in Toronto, when the guy next to me was shot in the shoulder by a stray bullet. That was God covering me. The situation could have easily been different. I remember being in a car accident, head on with a truck my uncle was driving. He ended up spending a few days in the hospital because of internal bleeding from the accident. I ended up with a hairline stress fracture, but walked away. I remember going to the junkyard where they towed the car after the accident. I went with my aunt (my uncle's wife) and a family friend. I asked the owner of the junkyard for the car and he told us that he was told that everyone in the car died in the accident . My aunt took one look at the car and almost fainted. Looking at the car after the accident I asked myself to this day how did I walk away from that accident? They had to use the jaws of life to get us out of that car. I knew then and there that God had his hands on my life.

I will never tell you to get yourself a sign and a soapbox and stand on the street and start yelling on the top of your lungs Jesus saves or repent the end is near, but I will tell you that your life must reflect what you believe and who governs your life. On your job, do your co-workers know you are a Christian? Do you have to tell them or do they notice there is something different about you because you don't gossip about other co-workers , you don't break out in an angry rage when things don't go your way or you're having a bad day. Do they see you praying? Witnessing is our ministry, as a believer witnessing should be a way of life, when you walk into a room your countenance, your attitude, your speech should say there is something different about this person. Some of us do not evangelize because of fear. We're afraid that our co-workers will ask us a question we can't answer, or if we approach a co-worker they might get angry. The way you will get over fear of evangelizing on the job is by sharing something encouraging with your co-worker every day. Start by showing the fruits of the spirit, love, joy, kindness, goodness, gentleness, self-control, peace, faithfulness, and longsuffering or patience. We must express these traits every day of our lives, not just on the job, but everywhere we go and with everyone we meet because you never know when you're going to get the chance to minister to someone and fulfill the great commission we were all called to do.

HOW TO DEVELOP YOUR MINISTRY

My early years were spent growing up with my great-great grandparents, they lived in the country-side on a large piece of land; we were a poor family. My great-great grandfather had a horse and buggy or as we called it mule and dray. Every year, he would tell the family what he was going to plant on the farm, around spring just before the first rainy season he would tie a plow to the mule and plow the land. For those of you who might not understand what I mean, a plow is a tool used in farming for preparing the soil for sowing seed.

The crops he usually planted were corn, yam, sweet potato, carrots, tomato, and banana etc. The first thing he did was to prepare the soil. Any farmer will tell you preparing the soil before you plant anything is the most important thing you can do. Another important thing you must do is find out what type of soil you have for those of us who are backyard farmers we take our soil for granted we believe that once it's soil we should be able to plant anything in it and it should grow,

in other words "dig a hole, plant the seed, and assume it will grow " while that may be true in some cases, the type of soil you have can dictate what type of harvest you will get. You might have to add more dirt or good soil to get the best crop or best results, meaning you must create the best growing environment.

I often think about my great-great grandfather and farming. As a believer, if you want all that God has for you i.e. reap the blessing and benefit, you must plant His word in your hearts. Some of us are coming out of some rough places, some of us should not even be alive. For some of us, because of what we have been through we shouldn't still be standing. The word says that HE loves us so much that He sent His son to die for us, it also says that nothing can separate us from His love. The word says, He has a purpose for each and every one of us. If you want to experience the manifested power of God in your life, then plant His word in your heart.

To prepare your heart to plant the word, you have to search yourself. Ask for forgiveness and ask Jesus to come into your heart, you don't have to be a Christian to be blessed, but to fulfill God's purpose for your life you must accept His Son Jesus Christ as your Lord and Savior. If you're looking for peace you must accept Him, if you're looking for unconditional love, you should get to know Him, and if you want to know what living water tastes like, accept JESUS.

Your home is your ministry, your marriage is your ministry, your job is your ministry, you are a walking talking ministry. God must have done something for you to minister about. Let your light shine, so men will see your good works and glorify the Father which is in heaven. Share your story and try to find at least one person per month to share the goodness of God with.

Not all of us will have the privilege to get to work in ministry. One of the best ways to share your faith is simply by being an example for Christ. Your life can be a true ministry. But, it works both ways. People will only be interested in what you say when they see the evidence in your life. People will quickly spot whether your spiritual life is authentic or phony. One of the best ways to show Jesus in your life is by loving others. Jesus taught us to how to share the gospel by showing our love to others (John 13:34-35).

Always remember your life is your ministry, and the Giants you face are your message
-Wilfred Brown

CHAPTER 15

THE SEASONS OF SOWING AND REAPING

I have heard it said before that today is the father of tomorrow. Everything in life starts with a seed. Faith is a seed. Fighting the good fight of faith starts with knowing you are precious in God's eyes and believing that your faith will produce good fruit. To begin sowing today for a brighter tomorrow, you start telling yourself: *you are blessed right now; you are healthy right now, you are a business owner right now, and your kids are blessed right now.* You have to believe what you are sowing before the evidence shows up. If I say, I am an apple tree, when you look at me, all you see is a tree, no apple, and if you look at me long enough, you might start thinking I am not an apple tree based on the way I look. But if I keep myself firmly planted in good soil and with enough water, you will one day see my apples, and you will then say "ha," he is an apple tree because you're now seeing my fruit. The trick to manifesting your blessing is first to believe that you are what you say you are, and eventually, the evidence, the fruit will show up, but first, you have to decide what comes first, the tree or the seed.

Who we are is the direct result of our thoughts. Our life is the reflection of how we see ourselves and how we have lived in the past. Those who make wise decisions will have the future they dream of.

> ***"Do not be deceived, God is not mocked; for whatever a man sows, this he will also reap."- Galatians 6:7***

Everyone understands the phrase "you reap what you sow" this principle applies to everyone, both Christians and non-Christians alike. The seed you sow grows the harvest you want, so sow seeds that will create the future you want. Listening is a seed, what you listen to most will influence what comes out of you. There are studies today that said that the music the kids are listening to today is influencing their language, their attitude, and their actions. It's even influencing their life choices. Your time is also a seed; if you don't know where you're going, serve someone that's going somewhere, read the story of Ruth and Naomi. Ruth was a woman that had lost everything and was told by her mother-in-law to go back home to her family and remarry . Still, Ruth must have seen purpose in Naomi and decided to follow her instead. Though Ruth did know where Naomi was going, and this was her response to Naomi's request, Ruth says, "Entreat me not to leave you, or to turn back from following you; For wherever you go, I will go; And wherever you lodge, I will lodge; Your people shall be my people, and your God, my God. Where you die, I will die, and there will I be buried. The LORD do so to me and more also if anything but death parts you and me." (Ruth 1:16-17 NKJV). She was willing to follow and serve her mother-in-law. God placed a Boaz in her life and fulfilled purpose. Are you willing to align yourself to the ministry God has placed you into so you can fulfill purpose? Are you willing to follow a man of God so God can use him to teach you how to be a Godly leader? Are you willing to sow your time in studying the word of God, so you can get wisdom as to how to be all that God has called you to be? Are you willing to listen to the mentors God has placed in your life to bring out the best in you?

When I didn't have money, I sowed my time, and my time was my seed. I sowed time because I knew the future I was trying to harvest. When I recommitted my life to Christ (at that time of my life I was broke), I had lost everything. I got divorced, a few years earlier I lost my business, and the bank foreclosed on my home. I was sleeping in my bed one morning when around 6:30 AM I was woken by the police shining a light in my face telling me I had twenty minutes to get all my belongings and get out of the house. I had to put everything out on the sidewalk. What made it more embarrassing was that I had a Pastor from New York, staying with my house. We were both out on the sidewalk in our pajamas. I thought my life was over. I didn't have any money, but like Ruth and Naomi I attached myself to The Faith Center and Bishop Henry Fernandez. I didn't know where I was going or what I was going to do, but God directed me to a man that knew exactly what he was doing and where he was going. I knew wherever God was going to take me went through Bishop Henry Fernandez, so not having any money I sowed my time as my seed. I volunteered for everything at the church. I was the first to show up and the last to leave and I watched God rebuild my life. He allowed me to reopen my business and I started to make a lot of money. I started buying and selling real estate, owning investment properties and other things. Then God blessed me with a virtuous woman and we got married. Because of the seeds I sowed, God moved upon my Bishop to ordain me and my wife as ministers in our church. I saw myself moved from the back of the church to the front row doing things in ministry that I never thought I would ever do. I learned to be a Godly leader in ministry and my home.

YOU CAN'T TITHE YOUR WAY TO A BLESSING. TITHING IS YOUR REASONABLE SERVICE. A SEED IS ANYTHING YOU INVEST INTO YOURSELF THAT WILL IMPROVE YOUR LIFE OR THE LIFE OF OTHERS AROUND YOU.

Don't put your money in the offering plate and think that God is obligated to bless you. God will bless you whether you tithe or not, but if you want to see the fullness of his blessing in your life, you must follow his commandments.

God has ordained seasons and cycles in our lives. Sometimes, when our dreams aren't coming to pass on our timetable, we get frustrated. But we have to be careful not to allow our attitude to keep us from moving forward. Understand that in God's kingdom, every season is not harvest. There are plowing seasons, planting seasons, and watering seasons. Sure, we would love for every season to be a time of increase; but without the other seasons, we wouldn't be prepared. It's during the plowing seasons when God is bringing issues to light that we need to deal with. He's getting us prepared for promotion. If you're not making as much progress as you would like, the key is not to lose any ground. Don't go backwards. Hold your position by keeping an attitude of faith and expectancy, even when it's hard. Keep plowing by speaking the Word daily. As you do, the harvest will appear in due season, it's coming!

> *As long as the earth endures, seedtime and harvest, cold and heat, summer and winter, day and night will never cease.*
> **Genesis 8:22 (NIV)**

LET US PRAY
A PRAYER FOR YOUR GREAT FIGHT

Father God we come in agreement with every person that took the time to read this book, you said where two or three are gathered you're in the midst, you will hear our prayer and heal our land we come in agreement right now that you will pour out a blessing upon us that our store house will not be able to contain. We will be like Peter, we will catch so much fish that we will have to give away, You said one can chase a thousand and two ten thousand so we chase the devour right now and declare us blessed to be a blessing, in Jesus name Amen.

ABOUT THE AUTHOR

Wilfred A. Brown is first and foremost, a husband to Inga H. Brown and a father to three beautiful children. He is an ordained minister and has been active in ministry for over 19 years. He has worked with his local government to better his community. He also works with some local churches to implement and develop Men's Ministries. He is a motivational speaker and a mentor to many. His mission is to merge local government and the church for betterment of the community. In addition, he keeps an active schedule in the area of his passions: Men's Ministry, youth mentorship, leadership training, and entrepreneurial workshops. His mission is to help people by empowering them to live their best life now.

CONTACT INFO:
Phone: 721-526-8798
Whatsapp: 754-308-0784
Email: greatfightgreatfaith@gmail.com
info@greatfightgreatfaith.com

www.ingramcontent.com/pod-product-compliance
Lightning Source LLC
Chambersburg PA
CBHW062038120526
44592CB00035B/1383